Love That Defies

Boundaries

Love That Defies Boundaries

Boundaries

A Heartfelt Collection Of Multicultural Love And Life Stories

AUTHOR: NIKITA GUPTA, MBA

EDITED BY: SACHIN GUPTA

www.growingupgupta.com

Dedication

This book is dedicated to each one of you that has shared your story on www.growingupgupta.com to positively impact the lives of others. Growing Up Gupta was created to provide visibility to unseen and unheard narratives of multicultural and multiracial people and families that you do not see in the mainstream media every day. This book unveils explicit, raw, and candid love and life stories from real people (whose names have been altered) that have prevailed despite all odds. May this book be a lifelong resource for you and your families.

Table Of Contents

Introduction

"I love you without knowing how, or when, or from where. I love you simply, without problems or pride: I love you in this way because I do not know any other way of loving but this, in which there is no I or you, so intimate that your hand upon my chest is my hand, so intimate that when I fall asleep your eyes close." ~Pablo Neruda

My Parents Only Saw Her Skin Color

After Sachin told his parents about his desire to marry Nikita, an African American woman, the result was a nightmare. Although she is intelligent and beautiful, they could not see past the color of her skin. His parents believed many of the stereotypes about African American women and people. Akin to how people in India immediately judge others by the fairness of their skin. And this created fights in the family that lasted for months.

Sachin would usually talk to his parent's multiple times a day, and now there was dead silence. Six months passed, and finally, Sachin's dad reached out to him. It would take years for his parents to accept their relationship and marriage fully.

Although his parents had come to the U.S.A. from India over 50 years ago, they could not fathom their son was marrying anyone other than an Indian woman.

On the other hand, Nikita had no challenges with marrying Sachin from her family. The first time she told her parents about Sachin, Nikita's father wittingly questioned, "what is a Sachin"?! Yet because her parents saw that he made her happy, they loved him from the start. Today, Sachin and Nikita have one daughter, Amaya, and Sachin's parents now call Nikita daughter too.

They have compiled this book because stories like this transform, inspire, and create a sense of community. This book of over 50 real stories by real people is for anyone dealing with the unique challenges of being a multicultural/multiracial person or in a multicultural relationship. Throughout this book's pages are words of advice, hope, and resolve.

Love Is The Most Powerful Force In The World

"Of all powers, love is the most powerful and the most powerless. It is the most powerful because it alone can conquer that final and most impregnable stronghold which is the human heart. It is the most powerless because it can do nothing except by consent."

~ Frederick Buechner

Standing The Test Of Time 30 Years And Counting

"Being deeply loved by someone gives you strength, while loving someone deeply gives you courage."

~Lao Tzu

Arshpreet is Punjabi; she was born in England. Her husband, Brian, is African American; he was born in Tennessee. They met at CVS Drug Store when it was called Long's Drugs. Arshpreet had been working there since high school. She knew Brian just transferred there, but he did not know she worked there. She walked in to buy something with her dad. When Brian saw her, he stood up. Then when he saw her dad in a turban, he sat back down.

Meeting Brian's parents for the first time was fine for Arshpreet. They might have thought she was too young for him, as they are 9 1/2 years apart (with him being older than her). Conversely, when Arshpreet took Brian to meet her parents, it was a problem. She was supposed to have an arranged marriage. Arshpreet's parents wanted her to marry a Punjabi. Hence their relationship ended up being a secret for seven years. Arshpreet lived at home the entire time because girls were not allowed to move out or go away to college back then. Consequently, Arshpreet lived at home through college and graduate school.

The inception of their romance was before cell phones and the internet's existence. So, their ability to communicate with each other was limited. All they could do was sneak a phone call from a landline occasionally. Arshpreet typically phoned Brian when she was at school, but she had to know where he would be. It would have been so much easier now with Facetime, texting, etc. For the most part, Arshpreet and Brian wrote super long love letters to one another, which had to be hidden or disposed of on Arshpreet's part.

Eventually, Arshpreet, told her parents approximately one month before finishing graduate school that she was going to marry Brian. It was not well received, and she would end up being disowned for six years by her family. They worried about what the East Indian community would think and did not want the family to "be shamed." Her mother had her take her to see Brian and begged him not to marry her. However, they knew they were meant to be together, and so they decided to have a small wedding at Arshpreet's friend's home.

Their Advice For Other Couples

- Be supportive of one another.

- Be generous and kind; do not give the family any reason to dislike you.

- Compromise.

- Act as a team.

- Be best friends.

After 30 years going strong one bit of advice that Arshpreet tells all the younger ladies, is to "Always be the girlfriend, not the wife," in marriage. Regarding the additional cultural obstacles, be patient and try not to get angry with extended family. Understand that this is all they know and that they are not yet ready to progress, but it does not mean that you cannot.

For those who are not the Indian partner, be patient with their families and with their ways of doing things. Indians are raised from infancy a certain way. The families will progress. Arshpreet's husband was always mature and confident in himself, only wanting her happiness. Therefore, he did not make it harder for her by fighting with her family. Over time, when you live lovingly with your Indian partner, your actions will show that you are happy and "good" together. Their hearts will soften. Grandbabies and old age bring change.

Faith And Love Made A Way

*"Love recognizes no barriers. It jumps hurdles, leaps fences, penetrates walls to arrive at its destination full of hope." ~*Maya Angelou

Ajey is Indian and Noel is Black. They are currently living in South East Asia. They truly come from two different worlds and upbringings. Ajey was born and raised in a very conservative Jain family in a small town in North India, and Noel grew up in a Christian family in Indiana. They met twelve years ago and got married in Nov 2015.They met in a Cuban salsa dance class in Texas. At that time, Ajey was a much better dancer than Noel. So, the first time they danced together, Noel stepped all over his feet. She was so embarrassed that she messaged him later that night apologizing. As time went on, they became friends, best friends. They talked about everything from their: hopes, dreams, fears, work, and families. Ajey introduced Noel to Indian food, and she introduced him to cheese and everything that contained sugar.

Neither of them imagined their friendship would turn into anything serious because Ajey was in the process of having an arranged marriage. Yet after they went to Cuba on holiday with a friend, things swiftly changed. It became apparent that they fancied each other, but still, they left it at that until they had "that moment." A moment at the airport when it was time for them to say goodbye to each other. They gave each other a long hug (the kind of hug you do not want to end), and then their eyes locked. It was like their eyes and heart spoke to each other without uttering a single word, and it was then that their relationship became serious.

Noel and Ajey never had that blissful "honeymoon" period couples experience when they first date because Ajey's family found out immediately through the grapevine that they were together. In Ajey's village, everyone has an arranged marriage. There are no if's, and's, or but's about it.

Hence when Ajey's parents found out, they were devastated and heartbroken. His mother had been dreaming about her perfect Indian daughter-in-law for years, and there he was, taking that all away. His parents could not understand why he wanted to humiliate them. They wondered what they did wrong in raising him. They regretted sending him to America to study. The biggest question was, "How could he do this to them?" Ajey, too, wondered how he could hurt the ones who sacrificed everything for him so that he could have everything. The pain was too much for him, his family, and Noel. On top of that, Noel's father was extremely disappointed because he envisioned her marrying an African

American man.

For the next four years, Ajey and Noel went through many ups and downs. Ajey's family continuously tried to push him into an arranged marriage. Then, he voluntarily took work assignments in Africa, followed by Europe, for over 2 years. He was running away from everyone because he simply could not choose between his family and Noel. How could he make such a decision? He avoided Noel for months (no phone calls, no emails, not texts) and did not speak to his family for a year. Imagine, how could two people simply falling in love and wanting to be married cause so much destruction to a family?

Nonetheless, Noel, aka Positive Pattie, never gave up. Instead, she decided to fast from her favorite comfort foods: French fries, gummy bears, and potato chips until they got married. It took 3.5 years from the point she began fasting for them to get married.

Additionally, Noel wrote note cards every night proclaiming that Ajey's family will accept them as a couple, she became vegetarian, and she took Hindi classes. To keep her sanity, she volunteered at a ranch after work and continued to take dance classes. She believed and had faith even when it looked like there was no way this would ever work. Ajey often told her she was foolishly optimistic. Her response was everything is possible. And she was right! When

Ajey's work assignment ended, he returned to the

United States, and they decided to move in together (which

they hid from both of their families). After spending so much

time apart, they wanted to make sure that this is what they

really wanted. They had many conversations about Ajey's

family's complexity, their expectations for a daughter-in-law,

and the possibility of them never accepting their relationship.

They also talked about how they would maintain their

relationship, knowing there could always be some sort of

strain or disappointment present.

Ajey eventually got the courage to introduce Noel to his

parents while they were visiting his sister in the United States.

He was terrified and worried about what he would do if they

did not like her. Noel was her usual "Positive Pattie self", and

their first meeting went well. They wanted to make sure that

this is what Noel really wanted. And if she could eat Indian

food and wear Indian clothes.

The following year, without Ajey's parent's blessings per

se, they decided to just go for it, and he proposed to Noel during

spring break in a small village in Italy. Ajey finally realized that

his parents would never say, "son, we give you our blessings to

marry Noel." Though deep down, he did want that. He wanted

them to be happy too. It was not

enough for just him to be satisfied. They were married later that year. Ajey's parents reluctantly attended their wedding, but they did and are trying to get to know Noel and accept her as their daughter.

Their Advice For Other Couples

- Pick your battles with family.

- Make sure your spouse is comfortable around your family. You must pick what comforts are the most important and deliver. Where Ajey is from, there is no such thing as "me time," "self-care", or privacy. These things are extremely important to Noel. So, when she visits his family, he makes sure she gets some "her" time every day, such as exercising, reading alone, etc. Noel also does the same for Ajey when they go visit her family.

- You can adopt another culture and still maintain your identity as well. It is hard not to throw yourself into your spouse's culture, especially if you are the one who is trying to win everyone over. Ajey does not have to be American because Noel is American, and she does not have to be Indian because he is Indian. They can be who they are while respecting each other's families and culture.

- Interracial relationships are hard, but they are a blessing at the same time. Most of the time, you will be going against the: wind, family, parents, society, friends, etc. Yet, you do not deserve a gold medal for dating someone of a different race, but you do get to benefit from your partner's experiences that could be significantly different from yours. However, for that to happen, you must continuously work on your relationship and push through.

- Celebrate each other's traditions while creating your own.

Love For A Lifetime

"Love is like the wind, you can't see it, but you can feel it."
~Nicholas Sparks

Amir is Indian, and his wife Grace is Chinese. They have two beautiful daughters, Mary and Gloria. They hail from the island of Singapore. Grace had signed up for a University's orientation camp in 2005, and days before the camp, Amir's friend – who also happened to be a senior and the camp organizer – called him to say they had too many girls and not enough guys signing up. So, he asked if Amir could do him a favor by joining the camp. Grace and Amir first got acquainted as members of the same orientation group. They were in a relationship after a mere 10 days together.

Shortly after they started their relationship, Amir and Grace both faced resistance from their parents for dating each other. However, they decided to study hard, and to get good grades together and they did. And this enabled their parents and those around them to realize that their love for each other helped them achieve meaningful things.

Their Advice For Other Couples

- If you are in an interracial relationship, you are bound to face resistance, no matter what you do or how nice you are. You cannot please everyone; someone is bound to be unhappy about your joy. Crucially, what others think about you is not as important as what you think of one another. The only good reason for you not being together should be if you find that you're not in love with one another, and not because your dad doesn't like him, or his mom doesn't like you, or something like that.

- Forget what looks right, forget what you think should be right, forget what your friends, parents, or others think is right, and ask yourself, "does the relationship feel right to me?" If the answer is yes, your relationship is perfectly fine.

- Find something fulfilling that you and your partner can share in and benefit from, that allows the people around you to see that you are serious about the relationship and not just out to have fun. For instance, you can help at a local charity, or do some community service together, or study and aim for good grades if you are in the same University. Also, take time to know and appreciate each other's culture and customs (a sure way to please your partner's parents). You will also find that the shared activity will help strengthen your bond further, which is another plus.

- Communicate with your partner often, about anything and everything, even the smallest and most random things. Amir and Grace still talk about random, pointless stuff, as well as important stuff, before they go to bed at night. You will find communication can really help strengthen a relationship, especially a marriage. Both you and your partner must commit to keeping that communication channel open all the time. It is vital, perhaps more important than any other aspect of a budding relationship.

- Finally, have fun! Interracial and intercultural relationships are lovely, for you get the best of two cultures, languages, and everything else, so it is double the joy. And if you settle down and have kids, you will raise engaging, deep, and charismatic multiracial children.

Our Love Is Worth Fighting For

"Love! Love until the night collapses."

~Pablo Neruda

Anil is Indian, and he was born in London (U.K.) and raised for the most part in California. His wife Jasmine is African American, and she was born and raised in San Diego, California. They met on social media and have been together for 18 years and married for 15 years.

Meeting Jasmine's mother for the first time was easy breezy for Anil. They initially met in the summer of 2002. Anil stayed at Jasmine and her mom's condo in San Diego, where they had a barbecue. Afterward, Jasmine and her friends took Anil to Los Angeles to celebrate his birthday. Her mom was super warm, friendly, and loving.

On the other hand, meeting Anil's parents was awfully hard and stressful. Anil's parents first met Jasmine at his M.B.A. college graduation, and they completely ignored her. Anil's parents felt withdrawn and out of place during the first meeting.

As a result, they would have to work together to convince Anil's parents that their love was real and earnest. His parents believed that Anil was merely infatuated with Jasmine. And they also questioned Jasmine's intentions and presumed that she would not learn or understand their culture. In spite of this, Anil and Jasmine stuck with each other through this arduous period by staying positive, strong, and devoted to each other. After sharing the news of their courting to Anil's family, they were utterly devastated that his parents wanted to disown him. After a year of grief, turmoil, and endless fights with his parents, Anil chose to stay with Jasmine. And he told his parents that they would lose him forever if they did not accept the situation. Within a few days, they invited Jasmine to their home in Kansas for a meet and greet. This ended up being a huge step in moving forward in their relationship.

Their Advice For Other Couples

- Be open-minded.

- Be supportive of each other's cultural differences. Stay ready and willing to step out of your comfort zone.

- Compromise and communication are key.

- Give your absolute best every day.

- Enjoy each other and be the best team player possible.

- Embrace the ups and downs as life is one big learning experience. Know that your love will be tested.

- Travel frequently as the beauty is in the journey and not the destination.

Getting Married No Matter What

"Love is divine only and difficult always. If you think it is easy you are a fool. If you think it is natural you are blind."

~Toni Morrison

Paul is Black American, and he was born and raised in TX. Ashima is Indian, and she was born in Punjab, India, and grew up in Texas. They met during undergrad at the University of North Texas in Denton, Texas, in 2010 through a mutual friend. Paul's parents embraced Ashima from the beginning. However, Ashima's parents had hesitations about Paul. He met Ashima's parents on multiple occasions as it was difficult for them to accept their daughter dating outside the culture/race, so it took them a while to come around. To date, their relationship with parents and family members is exemplary.

The obstacles that they faced made their union more robust. One of the first obstacles that they encountered were from people not being accepting of their relationship. Some things they, mainly Ashima, heard from people not being accepting of their relationship were:

- "The problem is that he is Black."
- "He's going to leave you."

- "He may meet all the criteria and be good in other aspects, but he's Black."

- "She's crazy for doing this; she must be an A.B.C.D. (American born confused Desi)."

- "Ashima knows a lot about her culture/religion; she knows how to read, write, and speak our language."

- "What you both have is not love."

- She's a Sikh, though; she's not Christian, so she believes in multiple Gods or what (in Sikhism there is One God), she's not Christian so she must worship the devil."

Together, Paul and Ashima had to stay strong and pray. When things like this were said, they had to explain repeatedly about who they are as individuals and as a couple. They could not and did not let this break them because they had already worked on and built a strong foundation.

However, a secondary obstacle they would face once they started dating is being in a long-distance relationship. Paul started his first job out of undergrad in California, and Ashima began the Physician Assistant program in Texas. Being long-distance was difficult, but they focused on communication and making sure they still worked on their relationship.

Their Advice For Other Couples

- Both people must be patient with each other.

- You have to be understanding about the relationship, personal life goals, and the type of relationship you are trying to build.

- Be committed and loyal to each other.

- Make sure to have open and honest communication about everything.

- Talk about the differences and similarities within the cultures, faiths, upbringing, and dietary restrictions.

- Communicate about how you will raise your children and where you see yourself as a couple.

- Do not ignore any of the issues mentioned above because they will come back, and it will only make things worse.

- Go to couple/marriage counseling or read marital books before getting married and continue to do so even after getting married.

- It may be hard at times, but you must stand up together and be 100% fully committed to the relationship.

- We are all humans with different backgrounds, but love does not see color, nor does it have any boundaries.

- No matter what your differences are or what outside negative noise, people are trying to project your way, keep working at it, and move forward.

- Most things are just negative and not accurate. So, ignore it, push through and continue to build the bond that you both have.

- If the other individual makes you happy, cares for you, takes care of you, unconditionally loves you, places God first in your relationship, is willing to work on the relationship, and is willing to choose you always, then nothing else matters.

Collectively, Paul and Ashima love learning new things, seeing things from a different perspective, learning new cultures, languages, fashion, foods, etc. They believe it shows humanity, love, and who God is. As humans, we are more than just our outward things. Love is beautiful. Love is worth it.

We Belong Together

"Love makes your soul crawl out from its hiding place."

~Zora Neale Hurston

Deepak was born in Punjab, India. He moved to the U.S.A. with his family when he was around 8 years old. Elise is an African American woman, and she was born and raised in North Carolina.

They are complete opposites, but they complement each other well. For example, Elise is more free-spirited, and Deepak is rigid. He is unbelievably stubborn. Elise is open-minded and willing to try new things. Deepak lives life by a strict schedule, and Elise goes with the flow. Their differences cause some friction, but they always find a way to work through it or laugh about it.

Elise and Deepak met in college while pledging the same co-ed business fraternity. Their pledge class was close, so they spent a lot of time together as a group. The following year, Deepak and Elise began to hang out one-on-one but just as friends. They had a great time going to the movies or grabbing a bite to eat, and their friendship blossomed quickly.

They attended a minor league baseball game in the summer of 2010. Elise confessed that she was interested in him romantically. He agreed that it was worth exploring. They called it quits, not long after, when he gave Elise some unsettling news. He informed her that his parents expected him to have an arranged marriage, and he feared that his family would disown him if they found out about her. Elise did not want Deepak to deal with that type of pressure or loss. She also refused to be his partner knowing that he already planned to marry another woman. They tried to remain friends, but their friendship was not the same. They ended their friendship as well.

Then, during the fall of 2012, Deepak re-entered Elise's life. They picked up right where they left off. By March of 2013, they started officially dating again. Elise was willing to make it work if Deepak was willing to fight for their relationship. They were finally on the same page. The arranged marriage was not an option anymore. Although Elise knew the choice was not easy she was grateful that Deepak wanted their relationship to flourish as badly as she did. Deepak proposed to Elise on the campus of North Carolina State University, where their complicated love story began. It was the best surprise of her life.

In order to get her to campus without spoiling the surprise, her cousin, Sabrina, decided that a photoshoot would be a good cover up. She convinced Elise that she needed her for a photoshoot for her photography business.

Elise dislikes being photographed, but she adores her cousin, so she agreed. If she had to be a part of a photoshoot, she needed reinforcements. Elise enlisted her friend Bethany to be in the photos as well. It turns out she was in on the scheme.

Sabrina, Bethany, and Elise arrived at her favorite area of campus, the Court of Carolina, for this photoshoot. It was dark out, so Elise was confused about how they were going to get any good pictures without natural light. She saw rose petals scattered on the grass. A white poster board was set up along with a projector. And before she could even gather her thoughts, tears of absolute joy began to fall, and Deepak was on one knee.

Their engagement was so special, and a complete dream come true. Elise calls it the night of answered prayers. She knew for a long time that she wanted to be Deepak's wife. It was just a matter of him asking her. The night was full of moments that she'd treasure forever, and thanks to her cousin, she has photos of those moments as well.

Deepak's mother and older brother attended the engagement. Elise cannot even describe in words how amazing it was to finally meet them. Deepak also made sure her immediate family members and their closest friends witnessed such a massive milestone for them. Elise "ugly cried" the entire time, and her heart overflowed with joy.

Deepak and Elise are now happily married.

Their Advice For Other Couples

- Do what is best for you. No one else will have the answers for you.

- Expose your partner to your culture.

- Be honest and open with your partner throughout your relationship.

- If you decide to go against tradition or your family's wishes, prepare yourself and your partner for the worst and best-case scenario.

- Know that you are not alone. It might be helpful to find other couples that understand what you are going through.

Open To Love

"When our heart is open. Everything we do becomes love." ~ Mimi Novic

Gauri is South Asian, and her husband, Henry, is Black. They were born and raised in San Diego, CA. They met through a mutual friend. Gauri had never dated a Black man, and Henry had never dated an Indian woman, but they were both open to love outside of their cultures.

Therefore, it was nerve-racking for Gauri to make the best impression on Henry's parents. They grilled her on everything, but they did not think that the relationship would last.

For Henry, meeting Gauri's parents caused many questions to be raised about how their cultures could coexist. Henry made himself an open book. At the end of the day, both families were leery that their union would last, but they have been married for over 11 years.

Undeniably, it has taken some time for them to build a relationship with each other's parents. They both had to dismantle the stereotypes that are associated with their respective cultures. Additionally, they had to substantiate their love to their families.

Henry found that South Asians can be a very

unwelcoming group. Often not wanting to accept outsiders. Gauri found that Henry's family was very protective and close-knit. They did not welcome outsiders into their family unless they affirmed that they would be suitable for the family. Nonetheless, through consistency, attending family gatherings, and spending time together they have built an unbeatable trust.

Their Advice For Other Couples

- Be open to the things you do not understand.

- Learn to accept the things you cannot change about your partner's family. Make sure you discuss the significant issues of marriage, kids, family celebrations, and dreams before getting married. It saves everyone from a lot of grief and discomfort later down the road.

- Do not be afraid to have hard conversations.

- Always be calm.

- At all times, try to put yourself in your partner's shoes.

- Remember to laugh and breathe because nothing lasts forever.

- You are both on a journey together.

- Find happiness in the small things.

- Never forget to laugh or smile with each other.

- Enjoy each other's company because it can help you get through the toughest of situations.

Henry and Gauri love how diverse and colorful their marriage makes their family and world. They are still learning the importance of living life on their terms. And could not have found a better life partner in each other.

My Parents Were Not Comfortable At First

"Darling, if it isn't you, it isn't anyone."
~Unknown

Tracy is Indian, and she was born and raised in the Middle East. Her husband, Woodrow, is Black, and he was born and raised in Detroit, MI. They met on a dating app.

Woodrow's parents were enthusiastic about meeting Tracy, but her parents were initially not keen on meeting Woodrow. They had expressed to Tracy that they preferred that she did not marry him because they felt that their cultural differences would only cause tension in their marriage. They were also genuinely concerned about what other people in the community would think about Tracy as the union of Black and Indian ethnicities is not commonly seen in her community. They also had their reservations about him because of negative stereotypes they believed about Black men. Yet, after they met him, they liked him, but there would still be many things that they had to unlearn as a mixed couple.

Tracy comes from a very collectivistic family background. On the contrary, Woodrow comes from an individualistic family background. Thereby, Woodrow can make decisions without asking for others' permission all the time. On the other hand, Tracy was raised to ask permission or get approval before moving forward with any decision. With this said, they struggled with Tracy's parents' acceptance of her marrying someone outside the Indian community.

Their Advice For Other Couples

- Respect each other's boundaries and try to be more understanding of each other.

- All obstacles will not have a resolution, but constant communication with each other helps.

- If you are a believer, then lean on your faith in God.

- Be mindful of any expectations you have before you get married, and make sure it is discussed with your partner since there may be many cultural differences.

- Be willing to learn about different aspects of your partner's culture.

- Respect each other's beliefs and ideologies even if you disagree with it.

- Respect each other's families and their values.

- Do not dismiss anything (about each other) because you find it unimportant personally.

- If your parents disapprove of your marriage, know

that although your parents love you and want the best for you, sometimes their "best" can be clouded by their desires to gain approval from others.

- Do not be afraid to seek counsel from professionals or anyone else who can help you. You are not alone!

Today both Tracy and Woodrow love that they are always learning something new about each other. Although they know they may never fully understand each other's struggles, they will always listen and support each other. Currently, Tracy is gaining a greater understanding and awareness about what it is like to be a Black man/person in the U.S.A. And they cannot wait to teach their future children her family language. Funny enough, they both thought that interracial marriages must be so much more complicated, but any marriage requires personal sacrifice to pursue unity.

Until We Meet Again

"Culture opens the sense of beauty."
~Ralph Waldo Emerson.

Aditi is Indian, and she was born and raised in Bangalore, India. Her husband, Thomas, is White, and he was born and raised in New Jersey, U.S.A. Aditi moved to the East Coast, in the U.S.A., for work. Her first day on the job, a charming, good looking, down to earth man walked up, said hi, and sat next to her. His name was Thomas. Aditi would tease him about all the girls "dropping by to say hi," and they would chat about cricket, surfing, and more. To her surprise, Thomas even knew a few Bollywood songs. Shortly after that, he relocated to the West Coast of the U.S.A. for work. Three years later, Aditi moved to the West Coast of the U.S.A. for a promotion, and they reconnected. A few years later, they started dating and eventually got married. Today, they are parents to two adorable fur kids and one delightful human baby.

Aditi's parents raised her to forge her own path in life and to think for herself. So, when they met Thomas, they knew she had made the right choice for herself, and they joyfully overfed Thomas Indian food. Thomas was not allowed to say no, because it is considered impolite in Aditi's culture. Similarly, Thomas's parents were kind, generous, and uplifting to Aditi. Thereby, building a relationship with each other's parents was not tricky, but they made time to invest in the relationship. How? By doing things such as:

- Making weekend calls to each other's parents.

- Sending flowers just because.

- Providing updates on the kids.

- Appreciating & adopting the traditions that both families are keen to pass on.

Their Advice To Other Couples

- Figure out what is most important to each individual and take the time to help your partner understand "the why."

- Have an open mind, and truly accept the differences. Isn't that what empathy is all about?

Rightly so, Aditi and Thomas love the beauty of their differences and how life is never dull. Additionally, they love the different traditions, big and small, including the thoughts behind them, the stories, the reasons, and the smiles they bring to people's faces. As well as the fantastic way it connects generations.

Against All Odds

"When two people are meant for each other, no time is too long, no distance is too far, no one can ever tear them apart." ~ Unknown

Sheweta is Indian, and she was born in Kerala, India. Her family moved to New Jersey when she was three years old. Will is African American, and he was born and raised in New York.

Will and Sheweta met in New York City, NY, more specifically, the Lower East Side. They were both patrons at a restaurant called Beauty and Essex. Sheweta was with one of her best friends, and they had just met up with her after a long week of law school. She had just gotten her hair done and wanted to enjoy a nice night out before going back to studying the rest of the weekend. Will, on the other hand, had also just finished an intense work week and happened to stumble into the restaurant. He had no preconceived idea to go there that night, but the energy of New York City's randomness brought him in. They made a genuine connection that evening and found themselves being friends for more than a year before dating.

The first time Sheweta met Will's parents was on a Saturday in October; they had driven down from Upstate

New York. They spent the day walking around 34th street and took them shopping at Macys. They finished the day at a nice restaurant and had a fun-filled day together.

Will initially met Sheweta's father and brother on a sunny Saturday afternoon in April. They had lunch together. They were more than curious to find out who Sheweta was spending her time with. In addition to why she was not coming home on the weekends as much. During that time, her family expected her to travel back home, most if not every weekend, to attend church events and to focus on the immediate family. When Will and Sheweta started seriously dating, Sheweta limited the time going back home because she wanted to spend as much time with Will as possible.

Truthfully, it was a challenging and emotional meeting; they were very abrasive and challenged Sheweta's desire to be with Will over the family. They explained that the relationship was growing, and they were happy. They tried to communicate that they wanted to maintain or even develop a more significant relationship with Sheweta's family while including Will. Unfortunately, her parents were not amenable to the idea and wanted Sheweta to stop dating Will immediately. At this point, they had not vocalized marriage, but their actions were resolute. To even get to the point that Sheweta told her parents that she was dating someone not

Indian but African American was a profoundly serious and calculated decision.

To this day, they are struggling with Sheweta's family accepting their marriage. Sadly, they have not spoken to them since their engagement (three years ago), and they are still actively trying to build a relationship. Unfortunately, they are not as receptive as they had envisioned.

As a result, Will and Sheweta are cultivating strong relationships and building a community of love with those that approve of their relationship. Will's family has been extraordinarily welcoming, and Sheweta's extended family has been more than supportive and loving to both of them.

Their Advice For Other Couples

- Openness, understanding, and curiosity are qualities needed to succeed in an interracial relationship.

- It is also important to be confident in knowing that both of you will be different and have cultural expressions that may not resonate with each other. Therefore, have the patience to explain and to welcome your partner into aspects of your life that might be foreign to them.

- Trust in each other, and hopefully, you will know early on that this struggle will be worth it in the future.

- Living an interracial/intercultural life is not easy, and it will be challenging at times.

- Communication is crucial, and it is essential to keep yourself grounded.

Never Lose Faith

"It wasn't until Amit went to India and talked to his parents face to face that they finally agreed to this union." Maria & Amit

Maria is a second-generation Cuban – American woman married to Amit, who is from India. They have two beautiful kids. They met in 2008 when meeting on the Internet was a bit unorthodox. After talking through social media for a couple of weeks, they learned a lot about each other. They came to know that they were both living in the same city and decided to meet. At the time, Amit was working for a company in Miami, Florida, while Maria was starting college. They had enjoyed spending time together and looked for any opportunity to meet. Not long after their friendship started did Amit ask Maria to be his girlfriend.

Their relationship was blossoming quickly, until it was time to tell Amit's parents about their relationship. They were then faced with the hardship of his parents not agreeing to their relationship. Even though this hurdle presented itself during one of the happiest moments, they kept a smile on their faces and continued to see each other.

It was not until Amit went back to India (during their year long-distance relationship) and talked to his parents face to face that they finally agreed to them being together. One thing that they never lost was faith that his parents would see that they were meant to be together.

Their Advice For Other Couples

- Talk about your value, and what is important to you. Coming from two completely different places, religions, and cultures, you want to make sure that both sides are always being represented. Now that Amit and Maria have children, they are teaching them about both of their cultures, traditions, and customs. In their home they celebrate Christmas and Easter as well as Holi and Diwali.

- Communication is key. Always ask each other's opinion, even on the smallest things. It is important for you to be able to figure things out together. Communication has the power to strengthen a relationship because it makes you feel valued.

- Food is such a big part of both their families. Food brings people together, and Maria secretly believed it was her cooking that ultimately made Amit fall in love with her. She still remembers the first time her In-laws came to the US. Amit had asked for Jalebi (an Indian sugar syrup funnel cake) for breakfast, and her in-laws were shocked that she knew how to make this from scratch like they do in India. Maria was ecstatic to make these for them because they speak little English so she cannot communicate with them through language but believes that food has a voice of its own.

Fate Brought Us Together

"If you're truly meant to be together, life will find a way to make it happen."
~Unknown

Manu is Indian, and he was born and raised in India. He moved to the United States of America at 26 years old. Stephanie is Caucasian, and she is a midwestern girl born and raised in IL. Together, they made Nashville, TN, their home for the last one and a half years, but recently moved to Louisville, KY.

Manu and Stephanie believe they were brought together by fate. Manu was traveling through Chicago on business and wanted to take the opportunity to meet with some Indian girls. He was proactively looking to meet someone before his parents could start setting him up on dates. So, by setting his dating app to 'Chicago' and 'Indian,' he thought his chances were rather good. Though Manu's filters kept Stephanie away, her dating app brought ;him right to her fingertips - a swipe right, of course. She wasn't exactly what he was searching for; as every Indian boy knows, if you're ready for marriage, it's time to settle down with a sweet Indian girl—one in particular where you both understand the customs and traditions of marriage by a certain age. But the redhead in the photos named Stephanie seemed intriguing, so Manu decided to match with her as well.

Their first date was as perfect as could be - a Chicago Ice Storm had kept the entire city home. Therefore, the dance floor and D.J. were all theirs at a downtown Salsa club. What could have been a terribly awkward experience turned into hours of laughing, talking, and of course - sexy salsa dancing.

However, towards the end of their date, the reality of the distance between them hit. At that moment, Stephanie decided that if Manu was ready for marriage and had come to the city to meet a compatible Indian girl, who was she to stand in the way? They were better just as friends who shared a fantastic first (and last) date.

Taking the goodbyes harder than they both thought, their Monday's back at work were equally terrible. With the date on his mind, Manu took a wrong turn driving to work. Meanwhile, Stephanie was deep in the doldrum and accidentally 'replied all' to a company-wide email. Yikes!

Eventually, weeks of phone calls finally grew into a budding relationship, and Manu found himself driving 8.5 hours to surprise Stephanie in Chicago to propose. Not to propose marriage but to formally make Stephanie his significant other with the intention of marriage in the future. Manu met Stephanie's family first during a full extended family birthday party. He fit right in because her entire family are world travelers. There was never a dull moment, and he felt very included. A noteworthy experience during their first meeting is that Manu ate pancakes for the first time.

Stephanie met Manu's parents five days before their wedding when they visited the U.S.A. for the first time. They had just purchased a house together and moved in 3 days before their visit. Meeting in-laws, getting married, and a brand-new home are all big steps.

Two unique experiences during their first meeting are that Stephanie taught Manu's parents how to use a seatbelt. If you have been to India, then you know they are not popular there. Secondly, Stephanie and Manu's mom had a blast draping sarees and sipping chai together.

Stephanie and Manu had to work through the arduous green card process.

Their Advice For Other Couples Going Through The Green Card Process

- Get started on the process earlier than later; no harm in gathering paperwork before the wedding date. Then all you need to do is plug in your marriage certificate.
- Keep a google photos file, and anytime you get a great picture with friends or holidays, just file it away

right away, so you have a great folder to choose from. When Snap fish or Walgreens runs a sale, you already know which pictures you need to print.

- Create a shared drive, so you both have access to adding W-2's, birth certificates, and all of the paperwork you need to submit.

- Once you submit your paperwork, keep it all handy in your google drive account as chances are that you will need it again.

- The interviewers can tell when you are in love, so don't worry about questions.

.

The Greatest Love

"Ruby's mother cried hard for nearly an hour.' She just insistently kept
saying, we don't do this…"
~ Bill & Ruby

Bill is an African American man, and he was born in Mt. Clemens, MI. His beautiful wife, Ruby, is Indian, and she was born in Bhopal, India. Bill lived in California for two years, other than that in S.E. Michigan his entire life. Ruby moved from India to Detroit, MI, when she was about nine years old. She lived in the city of Detroit, MI, for a few years and eventually, Troy, MI.

Bill and Ruby met on Sunday, June 30, 1991. He had just graduated, and his church had taken him out to eat at a restaurant, which was also Ruby's place of employment. It was Ruby's first day on the job that day, and she was so gorgeous to Bill. Bill's entire church had come in, so instead of training her, the restaurant decided to sit her down until "the rush was over."

While she was sitting there, Bill wanted to talk to her, but he was scared. So, he sent his friend to ask her for a few things: straws, spoons, extra napkins, etc. She was more annoyed than amused because she did not know where anything was. Finally, Bill asked his friend to ask her for her phone number. She sent back her answer. No! Bill was devastated, embarrassed, and humiliated, but he managed to eat. After everyone ate, they all left the restaurant.

Then just before, Bill left, he walked past Ruby, and she said that she would take his number. Bill was excited, so he gave it to her, and he walked out of the restaurant, excited. A few days later, she called, and they arranged their 1st meeting. After that, it was a wrap/they were together.

Nevertheless, Bill and Ruby had to sneak and date one another. Ruby told Bill early on that she was not at all allowed to date, call members of the opposite sex, or have a boyfriend. Her father had been killed by a drunk driver shortly after they moved to Detroit, MI, so she lived with her mother and two sisters. Therefore, they had to avoid the Indian American community altogether. They would meet at her friend's house about a half a mile away.

And after two years of successfully secretly dating, Ruby's mother's suspicions were validated by Ruby, and she came clean. Afterward, she called Bill because her mother had called her uncle over to take her back to India. When Ruby told Bill what happened, he went over to their new house to see if he could help in any way; when he arrived at the door, Ruby's mother cried hard for nearly an hour. She just insistently kept saying," we don't do this…"

Eventually, Ruby's mom calmed down, and they began to talk. It did not go well. As it turned out, Ruby's mom revealed that she had already chosen a suitor for her daughter. She bought the brand-new house that they were in, and she was going to bring him to live there once he married her. She circulated the man's picture, and Ruby was ultimately told that if she continued to see Bill, she would not see her mother or her younger sisters again (Ruby is the oldest child). Ruby and Bill talked, they cried, and they thought. Ultimately, it was Ruby's decision to make. Ruby courageously left with Bill.

Ruby's mom had (it seemed) made good on her promise. She had taken Ruby's two sisters, and she just vanished after a while. They could not understand it. She had just bought a house and then disappeared. As it turned out, Ruby's mom had to go back to India and settle things with Ruby's "husband-to-be family." To complicate matters, Ruby had to stay with a friend of theirs when her mom first left because Bill had not yet found his own place. Upon Ruby's mom's return, Bill was intentional in trying to have Ruby patch things up with her mother. But they would not have a significant relationship until Bill and Ruby had their first child in 1995. After that, Bill was tolerated, and Ruby was embraced by Bill's family.

Their Advice For Other Couples

- Proceed with understanding. There will be angst and ire. Yet understand the reason why you are bucking against a centuries-old culture! Think about it; you are probably the first African American man in the family ever. So, suck it up and exercise some understanding.

- There will be culture clashes. But understand why you were born on two different hemispheres and/or have two different family ways of doing things/thinking.

- Start your relationship as friends, as your foundation, and stay focused on what you fell in love with during your courtship.

- There will be a myriad of different relational challenges but proceed together.

Today, and 29 years later, Bill and Ruby are happily married and have four boys. For them, combining cultures for the benefit of their children was easily done after they had fully embraced each other's cultures. When Bill was dating Ruby, he would spend hours in the encyclopedia studying India. She was the first Indian person that he had met in his life. She was the first exposure that he had to Indian: music, food, people, clothing, and language(s), etc. To no end, Ruby and Bill both acknowledged to not allow one culture to be amplified over the other.

Ruby ended up embracing Christianity: although, she was born and raised Hindu. After her father passed, they would attend Hindu temples less and less. Bill was born and raised in the church, and he had been a "church boy" all his life. For Ruby, this gave Bill an advantage because they both have similar life values and even love. Themes such as purity and righteousness were themes that they had embraced through different religions, but once they had children, they could both model and teach their children together. And eventually, Ruby's mom converted to Christianity as well.

Their Must-Know Parenting Advice

- Teach your children both cultures and be intentional about it. Make sure they watch movies and listen to music from both cultures.

- Begin and keep your own family traditions.

- It may not be all bad that your children to see you struggle and disagree, as well as make-up and keep loving one another.

I Choose You

"If I could choose you again, I'd still choose you." ~Unknown

Naomi is an African American woman. She was born and raised in Denver, Colorado, and lived in the same house for nearly 27 years. Her husband's name is Vipul, and he is Indian. Vipul was born and raised in Malaysia. Once they were married, they decided to make up their own last name since they do not have last names in Malaysia. Their new last name is Shermanathan.

So how exactly did up with their new last name? Their last name is a combination of both of their last names. Naomi's last name is Sherman, and in Malaysia, Vipul's name is his first name followed by his father's first name. There are many South Asian names that end in Nathan, Yoganathan, Swarminathan, Kanesanathan so they thought Shermanathan fit.

Naomi and Vipul met at a St. Patrick's Day bar crawl. The St. Patrick's Day pub crawl is a day event that you must buy tickets to. There are drink tickets for different pubs, and there are games you play to win more drink tickets or prizes.

Naomi's friends gave her their drink tickets to grab drinks for everyone. She must have looked confused because Vipul asked her if she was looking for the line to order. He let her cut in front of him in line while he was chatting about just moving to Colorado and that he was looking for people to hike with.

Naomi told Vipul she loved to hike and to be outdoors. They ended up exchanging numbers that day, and that was that. About a week later, they messaged each other and decided to grab some food. They met up and literally talked for 4 hours at the restaurant, and then they decided to walk around Downtown Denver for another 4 hours. Vipul was so cool and easy to talk to that they talked about everything, but Naomi was not in the mindset of dating or anything (they were simply hanging out). Then about a week after that, Vipul invited Naomi to do archery with his group of friends through Meetup. Naomi invited her brother and a couple of other friends, and they all had a blast. It was then that she started to admire Vipul.

When Vipul first announced that they were together, his mom was not happy at all. Naomi is not sure about what transpired, but she did know that he told his mom that this is his life, and she needs to respect his decisions. That discussion happened in 2014, and Naomi did not meet his parents until 2016. Vipul and Naomi went to Malaysia in 2016, and that is when she first met his family, and they were very welcoming and nice.

Conversely, Vipul met Naomi's family on a family hike. He was extremely shy and did not really talk, but it went well. Currently, they have solid relationships with their in-laws. Naomi's dad and brother are big motorcycle and car guys; they all recently went to the motorcycle track to practice their skills. And Naomi probably texts her mother-in-law (Athai) multiple times a week, and Athai and her mom chat all the time too.

Their Advice For Other Couples

- Discuss the dynamics of your family. Vipul's family is Hindu, and Naomi's family is Catholic, but when it comes down to it, their core values are the same, which is why they believe they work.

- Check-in on your core values together, they will change over time, and it is important to make sure both of your needs are being met.

- Be patient with each other; it took a while for them to genuinely open up to each other and get vulnerable and be honest. Frankly put, they are still working on being vulnerable with each other.

- Keep learning about each other's culture. Vipul is really waking up to what it means to be a brown person in America and how some people will treat you because of it. He never understood prejudice and racism until he came to America.

- Another big discussion to have with each other is about colorism that exists across cultures. In Indian culture, skin color is a big deal; Naomi had to "fight" with her makeup lady on her wedding day to apply makeup that is her actual skin color. The makeup artist was extremely sweet, but Naomi just did not think she understood.

Only Have Eyes For You

"The soul, fortunately, has an interpreter — often an unconscious but still a faithful interpreter — in the eye." ~Charlotte Bronte

James is a British Jamaican man, and Zara is a British Indian woman. They were both born and raised in London, UK. They met by chance on one of the most bizarre evenings. Zara was still mourning her last relationship. A relationship that was extinguished because their families were not accepting of the relationship due to religion. Her ex-boyfriend ended up having an arranged marriage immediately after they broke up. So, the moving on period had been nearly impossible for her.

As a result, her girlfriends frequently came over to get her out of the house. They knew she needed to be supported and reminded that her life was not over. Her usual way of coping was to go for a drive, and so they ended up taking a ride in her car. Zara did not even comb her hair, which had started to look quite matted and extremely messy, and she was still wearing her pajamas. So, with awfully messy hair, half-tied up in a ponytail, she put on a hoodie and grabbed the nearest sneakers and her car keys. Zara felt it was great to get out again with her girlfriends to talk and to laugh.

By default, she drove in the direction of where she would always meet her ex. And as she got out of the car, she realized there was nothing there. She was no longer that weak girl, and she deserved respect and someone that would fight for their love. Her girlfriends cheered her on as she got back into the car.

While driving back to her home, Zara noticed a light shining down from the sky into a vehicle. To this day, she cannot comprehend what it was and how she saw it from afar. Nonetheless, as she drove down the road, in the distance, she saw the side profile of a face in a car turning at the roundabout. At that moment, she said to her friends, oh my goodness, and her friends asked her what was wrong. Zara told them that "there is the most beautiful looking man that she has ever seen, and he is heading our way". Her girlfriends were shocked because she had not spoken of a man like this for over four years (since her ex-boyfriend).

Strangely enough, as Zara and her friends passed him, he gave her a look as he saw her. Her friends were super excited by how gorgeous he was, and they were all in the car feeling like teenagers again. One of her friends immediately said, go round to the exit he took, but Zara did not want to do that. Seconds later, her friend continued, what is the harm in it? Just go! So, they did. And as they headed towards the exit, he took, they saw that he was still there, and they continued to pass him without looking in his direction.

Surprisingly, as Zara looked into her rearview mirror there, he was following behind. And they were all giddy, and she felt rather happy because she had not felt a real giggle with her girls for a long time. Zara decided to park the car, and he parked and got out of his car. As he walked towards her car, she realized that she was still in her pajamas and her hair was undone, and she had no makeup on. So, she told her girlfriends to go for it, she was not interested.

Eagerly her friends watched him approach the passenger side of the car. He spoke to her girlfriends while Zara looked out onto the road. He then asked if "the driver has a phone number?" Zara felt like a little girl inside but responded by saying, "don't ask about me in front of me; talk to me directly!" It was then that she found out that his name was James, and he asked her for her phone number.

Zara refused several dates with James for a few months, and then they started to talk on the phone. Eventually, they became friends, and he made her laugh a lot, and she looked forward to his calls. And once she had fully grieved her previous relationship, she went on a date with James.

James' father lived in Jamaica, and he had been separated from his mother since he was a young boy.

Therefore, the first time Zara met his dad was via phone, and he was such a lovely and welcoming man. On the contrary, James's mother was not warm. She treated Zara like she was invisible, and she was bothered by their relationship.

With that said, James was incredibly nervous the first time he met Zara's parents at their house because her father was strict. As a result, he was meeting them as her friend, although Zara's mom knew they were dating. After the formal introductions were over, they did welcome James with open arms and treated him like a son.

Unfortunately, their journey has been grueling, and the pressure has been colossal. Zara's entire family, even the elders back in India, accepted James from the start and welcomed him into the family. Zara has no family in England except her mother, father, and brother. Thereby growing up as a child, her Indian community was also her family. In essence, she referred to her parent's friends as auntie and uncle and their children as her cousins since they grew up together. To her, they were all extended family members.

Yet, with the news of James and Zara's relationship and her becoming pregnant with their daughter, Isha, her parents were outcast and ill-treated by the Indian community. What should have been a joyous time turned into a living hell! Except for a few school friends, the friends/cousins that she had her entire life shunned her and said dreadful things about her.

To make matters worse, when their daughter Isha was a month old, she suffered brain damage and was in a coma. Doctors told James and Zara that she would be disabled or never walk or eat solids. During her hospitalization, James's mom and family (four siblings and kids from a prior relationship) in the U.K. provided no support. And they showed the same callousness when Zara miscarried their son and struggled with a horrendous battle with cancer lasting over two years. She was told she would not live (and ended up losing twins after her cancer diagnosis).

Still, there were no calls, texts, or visits by James's family. Instead, they had left Zara and Isha for dead. Afterward, James's mother did openly admit to her racism, and his family in the U.K. have never accepted Zara or their child because they are not "Black."

Through the trials, James and Zara count their blessings. They lean on Zara's dad and brother for unconditional love and support. James's father, who was their only support on his side of his family, passed away in 2010. And Zara's mom passed away in 2013, and they were both strong pillars for their union.

Altogether, every single one of these experiences and

many more brought them together. They made them stronger. James, Zara, and Isha are the three musketeers, as they like to say. Without a doubt and through it all, they believe that love conquers all time and time again!

Their Advice For Other Couple And Families

- Do not worry about what others think or what they will say about you.

- Love openly and from the heart.

- Go with your gut.

- If the relationship feels right, then you know it is correct.

- Other people do not make your marriage or your future.

- Remember, those who genuinely love you will support you because they want you to be happy.

- Embrace each other completely.

- Embrace both cultures. It is so important to take the time to understand each other's cultures or backgrounds.

- Communicate every step and help each other on the journey.

- If your love is true, the world and their opinions do not matter. Never sacrifice your happiness or your soul mate for society because society will always have judgment.

James and Zara have been in love for over 20 years. As her father has said to her, they have not killed anyone or done anything illegal. What is their crime? Falling in love is not a crime.

It Was Complicated But Worth The Wait

Megan is Caucasian, and she is Jewish. Sandeep is Indian, and he is Hindu. They first met the day Megan moved in the dorms at University of California, Sandeep was her Resident Assistant (RA). He was the cool senior with a charming smile that her freshman self-fell in love with. Megan's mom helped her move in and made her talk to him to ask for directions to her classes; little did she know what she started.

They dated casually for the next 4 years, but they were never in a serious relationship at that time because Sandeep felt he needed to be with an Indian girl ultimately. Eventually, they ended things for good, or so Megan thought. After a 9-month break, Sandeep came back into her life. He had told his family about Megan and wanted to make their relationship work regardless of the expectations people had (and that he had himself) of who he should be with.

Their Advice For Other Couples

- Being in an interracial/interfaith relationship keeps things fun and interesting.

- Bond over your commonalities. When they go to Sandeep's family functions, the adults mostly speak Gujarati, and it can be difficult to communicate with them. Because Megan is a vegetarian, and most of Sandeep's family is, they bond over the commonality of food.

- Observe holidays from both of your family's faiths. During last Hanukkah, Sandeep was traveling for work and Megan was bummed he was not going to be home to celebrate their first Hanukkah together. He surprised Megan by giving her sister 8 gifts to give to her every night. They even sang the prayer over FaceTime, which was the best part – seeing him try to pronounce the words. Although they both do not consider themselves particularly religious, they try observing holidays from both faiths.

We Are A Match

"His parents were sitting in his apartment watching Spike Lee's, Malcolm X, when she entered the room." ~Serena & Jai

Serena is African American, and Jai is Indian. They met, in person, at a Borders bookstore after first connecting on Match.com. Serena had no idea who she was meeting because she was not on Match.com for that long; Jai also used his real name when he emailed her. She went to Borders bookstore, assuming she would be meeting a Black man. And immediately to her surprise, this South-Asian man, she "winked" at, was there.

Jai was excited for Serena to meet his parents. Candidly, she still was not sure if she was that serious about him yet. His parents were sitting in his apartment watching Spike Lee's, Malcolm X, when she entered the room. Serena was cynical and thought it was staged. His mom hugged Serena, and so did his dad soon after. They gave the best first impression.

On the other hand, Jai met Serena's mom by accident- as he was dropping her off from hanging out. It was uncomfortable because it was not planned, and they were still getting to know each other. Serena's mom and her impromptu pop-up broke the ice at least. Her mom liked him and did not have an issue with his ethnicity. Both of their families know their ancestral kinship is deeper despite the barriers.

Their Advice For Other Couples

- Know your non-negotiables. The best thing Serena did, was set her boundaries with Jai early on. They talked about things that made each other uncomfortable about the other's racial and overall background.

- Consider the way you were brought up could be completely different and figure out a way to compromise or create a new way of living in harmony. They are from two different: spiritual, class, educational backgrounds, etc. They took the things they liked and discarded the things they did not to form their own way of living.

- Celebrate each other's culture by attending events, listening to music, cooking each other's food, and then find the connections between them. They played games and music that have elements of both cultures at their wedding.

Serena and Jai have two beautiful children. These are

their must-know tips for raising multicultural kids.

Their Advice For Other Parents

- Be equal in teaching your child about their ancestry. If they learn a language derived from India, learn one from the African diaspora.

- Mesh both cultures and religions, so they have a well-balanced view of who they are.

- Never speak from your negative experiences and project that on your children. If you did not have the best outcome with dating or marrying your racial counterpart, do not project that perception onto your children. That does not help bring us together as humans wanting to be accepted. Speak love, be love and give love.

- Lastly, how you love yourself, in the skin you are in, will be the way they will love themselves. Have images around the house that celebrate them. Toys, books, and movies should always reflect their beauty. Images have power!

Love Is Tender

"You never lose by loving. You always lose by holding back."
~Barbara de Angelis

Ella is a Caucasian woman from the U.S.A. Arya is an Indian man from India. They met on Tinder. People are often shocked when Ella tells them that she met the love of her life on a "hook-up site," but it is the truth. Their first date did not go well because every place they wanted to dine at was closed (it was a Sunday). Hence, they ended up in a dive bar, only to be interrupted by Ella's very obnoxious co-workers that evening (it is a small world). Arya handled it with immense kindness, and she was drawn to him.

From the moment Ella's mom met Arya, she loved him. Her entire family adores him as well. He is very nurturing towards the children in her family, which her grandmother fawns over.

Arya's parents are in India, but Ella has met them via Skype. Arya told them they were getting married, and they do not speak English. They had many questions. It really felt like an interrogation. They asked Ella why her parents are divorced and how she would communicate with them?

As a result, Ella and Arya contacted their friend Shashi for help with all of the unexpected questions. Shashi is a

South Indian woman married to a North Indian man, and they consider their marriage to be intercultural. Their families nearly disowned them for their love marriage, and they ended up giving Ella and Arya fantastic advice on how to deal with his parents and families since Arya's parents disapproved of them being together. Yet, with time they did approve of the relationship, and now Ella and Arya are married.

Their Advice For Other Couples

- Communication. Cultural differences are often caused by a misunderstanding/misinterpretation that leads to an argument. For example, Arya can say things that Ella takes very personally when his intent is not malicious at all. Assuming is the worst in this kind of relationship because the mind can go straight to the negative. Therefore, they had to learn to tell one another how they are feeling and listen without judgment.

- Compromise. They learned early on that in order to make this work; they would need to compromise. Where would they choose to live, the US or India? Would their future children be raised Hindu or Christian or a combination of the two? Would they have an Indian wedding in his homeland or a western ceremony here? These are all critical questions that must be answered. They thought of what is important to them, and after endless discussions, they figured out a way to combine what they both value.

- Find your own way as a couple. They had to learn to find their own path in their relationship. They are doing things the way they want to, and that is not going to change. Westerners and Indians will give a lot of advice on how your relationship should be, but it is about listening and then deciding for yourself.

- Both Ella and Arya are increasing their patience with each other. They have learned despite the cultural differences; they are two people that love being around each other. The ability to laugh at each other and themselves through little irritations is one of the foundations of their relationship. They have found that they are evolving, learning, and navigating together through this love.

From The Moment We Met

Veronica is biracial. Her mother is African-American, and her father is Caucasian. She was born and raised in a tiny state called New Hampshire in the USA. Her husband, Aarul, is Bengali. He was born in New Delhi, India, and raised in Kolkata in the State of West Bengal in India.

Veronica went to visit her cousin in upstate New York, 3 hours from New Hampshire, where she was living at the time. Aarul was living in the same town, studying for his Ph.D. A few years prior, he had come to the USA to study for his master's degree. And so, while Veronica was waiting for the other girls to get ready to go out for drinks and dancing, she decided to go on Tinder.

Veronica did not know why she went on Tinder, because she was leaving the next morning and would not be coming back for a long time (at least she thought so). Yet both she and Aarul swiped right. He ended up coming down to one of the bars, and they continued to see each other on the weekends and take vacations, for a year, before deciding to live together."

Veronica asked Aarul at the beginning of their

relationship if his family would be okay with their relationship. He told her that his mom would have no problem. She was relieved. Aarul's father sadly passed away before they met, but he believes that his dad would have really liked her. For the first two years of their relationship, Veronica would talk to her mother-in-law on the phone sometimes, and they would video chat occasionally; she even sent her some gifts. This past December, they finally went to India, and Veronica was welcomed with open arms. Her mother-in-law, her sister-in-law, and all Aarul's relatives are so kind and loving. Veronica feels like she gained a second family, and she looks forward to revisiting them.

For Aarul, the first meeting with Veronica's mom involved a 15-minute interrogation regarding his intentions with her beloved daughter. It was all slightly unnerving but well-intentioned. Her dad was jovial and even made Aarul help him install his new cooking range, the first time they met. Overall, Aarul enjoyed seeing that Veronica's parents cared about her and were discerning about the people she associated with.

Their Advice For Other Couples

- Hire a great lawyer if you are going through the green card process. After Aarul left his student visa status, they had to file for his green card, so they could live together in the USA. Luckily, their process was super easy compared to a lot of other immigration cases.

- Work to learn each other's languages.

- Be open and curious. We are all shaped by our experiences and upbringing; we respect and embrace the diversity that comes from it. Veronica loves that she gets to call India her second home and that she gained another family. Before meeting Aarul, she had tried southern and northern Indian food, but she had never tried Bengali food. It is quite different, but she loves it.

Veronica and Aarul love that they get to learn another language and celebrate so many different holidays. Furthermore, for Aarul the relationship opened up a new world of food and culture on one hand; on the other, it brought him exposure to the story of the Jewish and African American struggles of Veronica's ancestors.

Growing up in different countries and cultures, there are minute differences in body language and manners of speaking that come up in daily life. They are still trying to acknowledge these differences and learn from them.

In a divided world, diversity is all the more crucial. Use the unique opportunity of interracial/intercultural relationships as a way of promoting acceptance, tolerance, and love.

Love Is Enough

"A happy marriage is not about how compatible you are, but how you deal with incompatibility."

~Lee & Denzel

Lee is Chinese and Indian, and she was born and raised in Singapore. Denzel is Nigerian, and he was born and raised in Nigeria. They met online. They both love dogs, especially Lee. Therefore, when Denzel reached out to her online, and she saw a picture of his dogs, they immediately connected, and rest was the beginning of their life journey together.

Lee had some relatives that were happy, and some that were shocked and not so forthcoming. Yet Lee and Denzel knew they wanted to spend the rest of their lives together. Therefore, with her parent's blessing, no one else's opinion mattered. Today, the relatives who were not forthcoming see the love they have for each other, and they have nothing but positive words to say.

Their Advice For Other Families

- A happy marriage is not about how compatible you are, but how you deal with incompatibility.
- It is not about being in an interracial marriage; it is

about being in love with each other that defines who we are as a couple/family.

- Understand that some people are still very closed-minded about interracial families.

- Always teach your children to love themselves.

- The relationship you have with your spouse and children is special. The colorful thing about your marriage and parenting is that you get to expose it all to your children. It will be fun and exciting to learn and grow together as a family.

Full Speed Ahead

"Do not seek the because—in love there is no because, no reason,

no explanation, no solutions."

~Anais Nin

Mona is a South Indian woman from Bangalore, India, and Steven is an African American man from the USA. They met in graduate school when she arrived in the USA to do her Ph.D. Mona happened to do her research in the same laboratory Steven was in. However, for the next 3 years, until he graduated, they were simply good friends, living independent lives with different people. It was not until their individual relationships started to disintegrate that they realized that they had similar values and ideas of what they envisioned for their lives.

Although they were both initially afraid of announcing that they were dating to Mona's father and Steven's mother, they were pleasantly surprised that they had accepted their relationship as their choice. They dated for about three years before Steven popped the question. However, as soon as he did, life took off at full speed.

A week after they were engaged, Mona's employer muddled the paperwork for her visa renewal and said she needed to head back to India indefinitely. They decided that they did not want any surprises and decided to get married in a small court ceremony in the USA. With an agreement that a year from now they would have a big wedding ceremony. A month after that engagement day, they were married, and 12 hours after the wedding, they found out they were pregnant.

Today they have the sweetest baby boy, and if they had expected life to slow down any, they would be wrong. They never did have that big wedding ceremony either, and when they think about it, they would not have it any other way.

Their Advice For Other Couples

- Ask questions and have the difficult conversations. Mona and Steven come from two vastly different worlds with two quite different upbringings. Their exposure to each other's culture before they met was very much through the loose portrayal of characters in movies and television. Clearly, that leaves a lot of room for assumptions, most of which are wrong. For example, Steven educated Mona on the aspects of African American hair, while Mona explained in detail how India is a melting pot of various religions and cultures. While he sensitized her to the socio-political issues afflicting America today from the perspective of a Black man, Mona informed him of the finer nuances of colorism in India. Often in their discussions, the chasm in knowledge narrows down, and they find similarities they did not even know existed.

- Accept the differences. It is certainly important to find common ground. Align with each other as it relates to your values and goals, which lay the foundation for a successful marriage, and to accept that there will be inevitable differences.

- For example, Mona's husband wonders how she must have her fix of Indian food after consecutive American meals, and yet without asking, he suggests, cooks, or brings home Indian food he knows she will crave. Furthermore, while her family is historically Hindu, she was brought up with the knowledge of other religions and the freedom to practice or not practice one of her choosing. Steven's family is devout Catholic, and they will not miss a Sunday mass. For Mona, it has been accepting this part of his identity and supporting it, even though she still may not fully understand it.

- Celebrate one another. Interracial/cultural relationships are wrought with challenges, but the love and respect that any two individuals bring to a marriage still supersede any existing biases. For them, it becomes especially vital to celebrate one another, their backgrounds, their upbringing, their lessons, their challenges, and especially their cultures. It becomes even more relevant to keep that celebratory atmosphere alive because they have a son at the intersection of their love and cultures. A son who needs to understand that he is a unique product of two people who work hard at preserving the sense of who they are and encouraging each other to be themselves so that he may have the best of both worlds.

And Then There Was You

"Before I met you, I never knew what it was like to be able to look at someone and smile for no reason."

~ Unknown

Lauren is British, and she was born in Wales, UK. Her husband, Hari, is Indian, and he was born in India. Lauren traveled to Delhi for three months to work in India, and on her first day in the office, she met Hari.

Hari and Lauren started dating a month or so after meeting until Laruen went back to the UK. However, three weeks later, Lauren traveled back to Delhi, India, and they have been together since then.

Hari met Lauren's parents in their home in Wales. They spent a week with them on holiday. He was extremely nervous before meeting them, but it was very calm and casual. They all sat together and spoke about everything. And in the evening, the neighbor, Lauren's sister, and nieces came to visit, and everyone was so welcoming to him. Hari proposed to Lauren a few days later.

On the contrary, Lauren's first meeting with Hari's parents was in their home as she prepared for their Indian wedding reception. Hari was out shopping at the time, and she went into the living room on her own to meet them.

Hari's parents do not speak English, so they talked in her (limited) Hindi, and his brother translated. The conversation was full of laughs and a lot of pictures shown of each other's families and her life in the UK.

Lauren was extremely nervous before meeting Hari's parents, but they put her at ease. They gave her gifts for the wedding and vice versa. Hari's parents immediately made her feel like part of the family. When Hari came home, they told him how lovely she was and that they were so happy that they were getting married.

Lauren and Hari's friends were incredibly supportive when they heard about their relationship. However, they had some people from work in Delhi, India that made it clear that they were not happy about their relationship, and she was made to feel uncomfortable at work because of it.

Additionally, they naturally get looks walking through Delhi, and people do stare. Lauren has had a few comments in India from Indian people who have assumed she is a prostitute because she is with an Indian man however, they do not let these things stand in the way of their love.

Their Advice To Other Couples

- Be patient with each other. Growing up with entirely different backgrounds and experiences will reflect throughout your relationship.

- Have an understanding of each other's cultures and family. There will be different mindsets and expectations ingrained but develop an understanding.

- Act as a team. Many people have been against their relationship. You cannot let outsider's opinions tear you apart.

- Enjoy the traditions. Each person will celebrate different holidays and festivals. Enjoy each of them!

- Compromise. There will be times and circumstances which are difficult. Find common ground.

- There will always be challenging moments being in an interracial/intercultural relationship. People will not always understand why you are together.

Love Is Blind

"Love has no color."

~ Jason & Mina

Mina is a British Indian woman from Yorkshire, England. Her husband, Jason, is from Ireland. They have been together for 13 years and married for 3 years. Jason is a Christian, while Mina is Hindu.

Jason and Mina met at the age of 18 while attending the same University in Liverpool, England. To be exact, it was at a renowned gay nightclub in Liverpool, England but on a midweek student night. They introduced themselves to each other on the dance floor while enjoying the music and cheap drinks. They had a great night and discovered that they lived on the same university campus for almost a year. Jason and Mina swapped numbers at the end of the night and realized they had a spark between them.

Meeting Jason's parents was a bit nerve-racking. Jason invited Mina to his parent's house in Ireland for the weekend when they were 19. Mina had no idea what to expect or how to act because Jason was her first boyfriend. Mina decided to just be herself, but she was nervous. Thankfully, Jason's parents did not interrogate her with millions of questions and they fully supported their relationship. They have always treated her like their second daughter from day one. The most important bit of advice that Jason's parents gave them was just to make sure nobody gets hurt. Because at this point, Mina's parents were not aware of their relationship.

Quite the opposite, Jason met Mina's parents under slightly unfortunate circumstances. This was at a point where she was extremely unwell in the hospital, and her parents had found out that she had a boyfriend after 10 years. Therefore, Jason ended up going to Mina's parents' house for lunch with his mother with a huge bunch of flowers in his hands. He told Mina on the drive over; he was so nervous that he pulled over his car and threw up as he did not know how the meeting would go.

However, he was welcomed with open arms, and Jason was instantly at ease and spent the day getting to know Mina's parents. Mina's parents adore him, and they could see that he was the one for her as he stuck by her through thick and thin. He made weekly trips over to England so he could spend time with Mina in the hospital and get to know the rest of the family. Now they live close to Mina's parents. Thus, whenever he can, Jason spends time with her parents. He often goes to watch football with her dad and helps her mum in the kitchen sometimes, which she thinks is sweet.

Their Advice For Other Couples

- "Love has no color."

- Tell your parents /loved ones about your relationship sooner rather than later. Do not keep it a secret for longer than you must. Unfortunately, Mina found herself having to keep their relationship secret from her parents for so long because she was afraid of their reaction but, she should have realized that if she was happy, they would be happy. The amount of stress upset, and, worrying caused her health to be affected, but thankfully the love and support she received helped her get back on her feet.

- Respect each other's beliefs/cultures and learn about each other faiths. Mina often goes to church with Jason on a Sunday, and he goes to the Sikh /Hindu temple when she goes to worship. They celebrate Christmas, Easter, Diwali, and other festivals – they really get the best of both worlds. And even after 13 years together, they are still learning so much.

- Get each other's families involved. In Mina's culture, when they have wedding functions in the immediate family her mother and father in law are always invited. Her mother-in-law even owns her own sari, which she proudly wears to weddings, and it is nice that she can also experience a different culture too.

- Introduce each other to different foods as soon as possible. Jason was born and raised in a tiny town in Ireland, so when Mina met him, he had never eaten Indian food before. Mina would make him different curries, and they would eat out so he could experience lots of different dishes. This, in turn, made it so much easier when he first met her parents and had dinner at their house -he loves Indian food now.

- Stay positive. There will be lots of trials and triumphs that you will face but, if you keep a united front and, keep communicating your relationship will be a great success.

We Fit Together

"In all the world, there is no heart for me like yours. In all the world, there is no love for you like mine."

~ Maya Angelou

Tema is Indian, and she was born in Canada. Her family moved to the UK when she was a toddler. Her husband, Raymond, is Jamaican. He was born and raised in South London.

Raymond and Tema both worked at Boots in Liverpool Street Station while they were in College. Tema was on the makeup counter, working for Estee Lauder, and Raymond was in the photo lab. Tema liked Raymond, but she knew that he would never make the first move, nor would she customarily. She realized that as an Indian woman, Raymond would not go there, and so she figured he needed a little nudge. Therefore, she told someone at work, who was a notorious gossiper, that she thought Raymond was cute. Inevitably fate ran its course, and they are now married with two beautiful children.

They have been together since 2008. Raymond and Tema got engaged in 2013, married in 2014, and had their children in 2017 and 2019. They have had many ups and downs, but they have grown together. Genuinely, they would not know what to do without each other. They are like yin and yang, they have different personalities, but together they create a whole and balanced energy. They don't have to try with each other. Instead, it is natural and easy, exactly what they imagined marrying their soulmate would be.

Tema was fully accepted into Raymond's family. However, there was some concern as to whether Raymond would be accepted into her family.

They didn't experience any real obstacles in the beginning. However, racism and people's real feelings recently became more apparent. And this is after twelve years of being together and almost six years of marriage. Right now, what has been difficult for them is people's reactions to them. People stare when they are out and about. Some of them try to jump over furniture to get a good look at their children. And others quite obviously get their friends' attention so they can continue to stare and talk about them. Frankly, they don't know what they are saying, and they don't assume that it is negative, but if you catch them on a bad day they will say something.

Overall, Raymond and Tema deal with any situations they encounter by standing united, moving on, and not dwelling on things. They believe that if their home is happy, then they are fulfilled. Everything else is just noise. Racism and judgments are more a reflection of the person/people making them.

Their Advice For Other Couples

- Make sure the person you are with has the same/similar values and principles as you. Because without a solid foundation, you will have difficulty creating anything of value. If you have this, you can literally get through anything life throws at you.

- It is important to discuss non-negotiables in a relationship at the start so you can see if your views align. Raymond and Tema have never really had any disagreements, thankfully, but the one thing that is difficult is their traditions at the end of life. Tema cannot ever imagine being buried, and Raymond cannot think of anything worse than being cremated (unfortunately, Covid-19 has had them talking about all sorts of things).

- If you are struggling because your parents do not agree with your choice of partner and things are difficult, trust yourself and trust your choice. If you both decide that each other is worth the backlash, you may receive, then go for it. It will make you stronger, and you will both grow together. People fear what other people will say about them if their son/daughter marries outside their race, but the truth is that people will talk about whatever you do.

Their Tips For Other Parents

Their children are something that they have had long discussions about. They know that when it comes to filling out those equal opportunity questionnaires, their children will have to tick the 'other' box. Therefore, they want to make sure that they never feel an 'other' or like they do not belong to one culture or the other.

Additionally, they will raise them to know that they are unique, and that is what makes them great. Also, they don't necessarily want to focus on the cultural/religious aspect but to focus on raising them as good, kind, honest human beings who know that their outward appearance does not define them. Furthermore, they will expose them to both of their

cultures.

Drawn To You

~ Unknown

Abha is an Indian American woman, and her husband; John is African American. They met in March 2014. John moved from Tennessee to California to pursue his master's degree in Psychology. The plan was to become licensed so that he could begin practicing as a psychotherapist.

Upon moving there, he searched for a job. Since he worked for the YMCA in Nashville, TN as a trainer, he figured he could easily slide into an open position within the YMCA in Cupertino, CA. Fortunately, he was able to get a job at the Northwest YMCA, and from there, he started working while attending school at Santa Clara University. A year and a day later, he went to work on a Tuesday afternoon proceeding through his usual routine. He typically cleans some of the fitness equipment and preps the gym for his incoming clientele.

As he was going around cleaning the equipment, he saw a woman running on the gym's equipment. For a good 10 seconds, he was unable to take his eyes off her. She seemed different, but more importantly, he felt drawn to her. He quickly realized that it was not her who was different, but his whole being seemed to be responding to the very beauty in front of him. He was acting differently. It was as if he had forgotten what he was doing during the 10 seconds he spent looking at her. John's eyes caught the sudden twinge of muscle in her neck as she turned towards his line of view, and he quickly looked down towards the cleaning equipment in both of his hands to shake himself from the paralysis her presence placed him under. John literally had to remind himself of what he was doing with the cleaning utensils.

After that day, he was on a mission to find out who she was. John went to the front desk where members badged-in, and he asked the manager who badged in between the time of 1:15pm-2pm. With a confused look on her face, his manager asked why he needed to know. He dodged the question with a statement pertaining to her potential job promotion.

Once John's manager finished the search, his eyes tracked toward the screen and with wide-eyes, and he saw the name of the woman who was running on the treadmill. He saw the name of the woman whose presence literally stopped his mind's natural, biological tendency to think. Her name was Abha.

While John was awestruck by Abha, what caught her attention was the way John held himself. His hands were in his pockets, and his steps were taken as though he did not have a care in the world. Abha felt as though he encompassed the characteristics she wanted to see in herself. He felt like the opposite of her. She told all her friends about him; "an attractive Black guy, in the middle of Cupertino?! You must be kidding!

And then it happened. Abha walked into the stretching room and began her routine, and John walked in and started to "tidy things up." There was no one else in the room. He looked over and asked, "Are you training to be in a marathon or something?' I just always see you on the elliptical – and haven't seen too many people enjoy it as much as you do." Abha laughed. He introduced himself. And that was how their relationship began.

John and Abha dealt with a lot of difficult conversations early in their relationship. Nevertheless, because of their: different cultures, their personalities, and upbringings, they still had some important struggles to work through in their three years of dating. John did a great job of learning how Abha's culture and upbringing impacted their communication within their relationship. However, because she was starved of African American culture in Silicon Valley, she found it challenging to understand his communication style – causing some frustration.

Moreover, John also placed assumptions on Abha because of her culture or her parents, which led to a lot of miscommunication. They would argue over finances, careers, parents and family opinions, cooking, and household chores. It wasn't until they started to realize that without taking the time to listen to each other and understand the other person's point of view, the arguments that arose would be impossible to move forward from. John and Abha, had and still have so many differences, but they are now using these differences to their benefit, to build a stronger relationship.

They believe the turning point came when they decided to get married. John wanted to propose, and Abha wanted him to get her father's blessings. So, he waited patiently for her dad – who was living in India at the time, to come home. Abha and John approached her parents about getting married together, and there was dead silent. Abha's dad said he thought it was best for them to wait until they were more financially stable. Her mom followed by saying, "But we love you, John." They were crushed but not defeated. Abha told John that no matter what her parents said, she wanted him to pop the question, and she would say yes. And he did.

On November 26, they got engaged, but their challenges continued. They had moved in together, but John had assumed this meant they would be getting married soon, but this was not what Abha had in mind. She wanted to plan a wedding in Nashville, TN, which meant waiting till October 2017. After a lot of back and forth, scheduled and canceled appointments with the county clerk's office, they finally had a small ceremony on February 25th. They became husband and wife without Abha's family being in attendance.

Abha had decided not to invite her parents to their wedding. Her parents were not happy about this; even though they did not want them to rush into anything, they had wanted to be present. At the time, Abha was standing up for what she believed was right – to get married no matter what her parents said, and she does not regret that. But she does regret not having her parents and sister present to witness the small ceremony. Abha believes it was only fear that held her back.

From that day forward, Abha's parents made every effort to welcome John into their family as their son-in-law, and they have never looked back. Today, they are blessed with loving parents, siblings, grandparents and extended family on both sides. They know there are many people out there still who do not, and will not accept them, but they are continuing to use every struggle to build a stronger foundation of marriage from which they believe will stem a larger social impact.

Their Advice To Other Couples

- It is wise to know why you are entering into an interracial relationship. If you see an "exotic" person or you are interested because of their ethnic background, then the relationship may prove harder than your reasoning.

- When you enter a relationship with another person of a different culture and/or different ethnic background, you are leaving the comforts of your own culture. You cannot expect the person to adapt to your own culture, nor should the other person coerce you to adapt to his/her own. There is a learning curve in interracial and intercultural relationships and marriages on what to do when as it pertains to culture.

- Both parties should want to educate themselves on the person they are dating simply because their culture may have defined them or still does. It is wise to check your reasoning for wanting to embark on an interracial relationship, and to have a humbled mind when it comes to the frustrations that you will face because of the difference in behavior, culture, and lifestyle.

Take My Breathe Away

"I have looked at you in millions of ways and I have loved you in each."

~ Unknown

Sarika was born in West Africa to Indian parents and grew up in São Paulo, Brazil. Andrew was born and raised in Connecticut. Sarika is Hindu and Andrew is Jewish. They live in Washington, DC, where Sarika pursues her Graduate studies in Marketing at Georgetown and waits for Andrew to bring home a corgi puppy.

Andrew and Sarika met their Freshmen year of College at American University. Still, they share different stories on how things went, but they knew that they were instantly attracted to each other. In any event, they are now married and celebrating both of their cultures and religions.

Their Advice For Other Couples

- Open communication. The foundation of any relationship is open lines of communication. This is even more crucial when you and your partner come from different backgrounds–cultural or otherwise. To make things work, you need to talk through what values are most important to you and make sure that your partner understands and respect those values. This is even more important as your building your life together. For example, if you want to have children one day, it is imperative that you talk through how you want to raise them and what values you want to instill. They found that talking openly about what matters to them, and sharing that with one another, not only brought them closer together, but allowed them to build a strong foundation for their relationship.

- Stay open minded - be willing to try new things. An important part of being in an intercultural relationship is to be open to trying new things and being willing to participate in each other's traditions. Everything from types of food to religious holidays are things that they like to share with each another. Andrew's spice tolerance increased over the years, and he now surprises himself (and her) when he asks for hot sauce when they go out for dinner. They also celebrate Diwali together, and had their first Hanukkah at home this past year. Being able to enjoy each other's cultures and traditions is particularly important to making an intercultural/religious relationship work.

- Find the similarities and cherish the differences.

When you enter an intercultural relationship, you will likely be shocked by some of the differences between your cultures. That is why it is important to not only talk through those differences, but cherish them, and find the similarities between the two of you. Sarika found that her Indian family, and Andrew's Jewish family shared a lot of the same values. Jewish and Indian moms are remarkably similar in the way they worry about their kids and take care of their families. One of the things that made a difference in their relationship was having their families get along. Family values are important to both of them, and when their parents first met—and liked each other— that helped to solidify their future together. Finding the little things that overlap between your two cultures, and religions will help bridge the gap and bring you closer together.

And Then We Met Again

"You are my today and all of my tomorrows."
~Unknown

Anoop is Indian (Gujarati), and he was born in Boston, MA. His family moved to Louisiana when he was around eight years old. His wife, Michelle, is Caucasian and adopted, so she is not sure of her heritage but believes she is Cajun-French. Michelle was born in Baton Rouge, LA, and grew up in Alexandria/Pineville, LA.

They initially met in high school. As Anoop tells it, Michelle was older than him in high school and way too "pink" for his liking. However, after college, life brought him back home, and he saw her at a coffee shop and reached out to her after that. Likewise, Michelle remembers Anoop from high school, but they did not know each other then. It was not until life randomly brought them both back to their hometown.

Meeting Michelle's parents was very lowkey, and Anoop felt welcomed. They sat on the back porch and had a few beers; it was great. Conversely, Michelle was beyond nervous. She knew how unprecedented it was to meet Anoop's parents so early on, and she was determined to get it right. A childhood friend of Michelle's had married an Indian guy.

Therefore, she reached out to her for advice on how to impress them. Her friend advised her to eat seconds of everything and to do the dishes. And to this day, Michelle still follows this rule.

Their Advice For Other Couples

- Layout your priorities and compare your values before you decide to get married.

- Talk about money and the uncomfortable stuff. You may not realize what's a deal-breaker until you do.

- It is essential to remain patient with each other, no matter what. Of course, there have been times where lines have been blurred because of how they were raised. Strive to gain insight from each other on these childhood differences. They will help you understand more about each other.

- Anoop loves how seamlessly Michelle blends in with his family and the sisters she has gained. On the other hand, outside of all the spicy, mouthwatering fusion food they create, Michelle loves all the traditions their collective upbringing has inspired within their family. In addition to becoming unafraid of dancing in front of anyone, let alone a vast crowd. Since being married to Anoop, she cannot help but jump in on the perfectly choreographed Indian family dances during reception performances. Without a double being part of Anoop's family and active in the culture has taught Michelle a lot about herself.

Work Romance

"Do not allow your fears to control your decisions in life." ~ Paul &

Divya

Divya is Indian, and she was born and raised in Chicago, IL. Her husband Paul is of African American and Jewish descent. They have a sweet and beautiful Black and Indian daughter.

Paul and Divya met at work. Divya is a pharmacist, and Paul was a pharmacy technician. By fate, he accepted an offer for a tech position at the hospital pharmacy she worked in. They started working together, hit it off right away, and became friends.

Divya's parents are both from Kerala, India, and are Catholic. They were liberal parents compared to her Indian friends' parents. However, due to certain stereotypes, she was not allowed to date certain races or religions (African Americans and Jews were among them).

After creating a beautiful friendship, they decided to "secretly" see one another. Divya was technically his superior at work, so dating and working together would be a conflict of interest. As their relationship became more serious, Divya decided to introduce Paul to her parents. Paul's mom already knew about Divya because he had Divya meet his mom while they were dating. There were no issues on his side.

Surprisingly, Divya's dad had no problem with her dating Paul, despite his ethnic background. Yet, her mom was a little hesitant at the thought of Paul. But once they met him, they loved him. They did hit a few obstacles along the way due to personal reasons. Those reasons were enough for her Divya's dad to threaten to kick her out of the house if she decided to keep seeing him. Forthrightly, these are situations that a young Indian girl, marrying for the first time, would reject if it was an arranged marriage proposal. But, once her parents knew that Divya was set on marrying Paul, there was no convincing her otherwise. Her parents soon accepted him as their own and treated him as such. Divya's brother and husband get along like brothers.

Fast forward twenty years later, and they are still together. Divya's dad passed away 17 years ago, shortly after their daughter was born. He was so excited about her and loved her deeply during the three short months he knew her. Divya's dad became the dad to Paul he never knew. Paul was devastated when he passed.

The obstacles they have faced during their marriage have been more cultural than anything. They faced many ups and downs as with any marriage. But it is the love and respect they share that has pushed them to persevere in their marriage and to cling to each other even tighter through the worst of storms.

If they had been closed off to dating outside their race, they would not have experienced the beautiful life that they have today.

Their Advice For Other Couples

Do not allow your fears to control your decisions in life. Follow your heart and face your fears. You might be surprised how unfounded they are and how much more amazing your life can be.

For Your Love

"Once I knew you, I never wanted to know anyone else."
~ Leo Christopher

Hannah is Caucasian-American, and she was born and raised in Pennsylvania, USA. Mukesh is Indian, and he was born and raised in different parts of India.

Hannah and Mukesh met at a friend's party in Washington, DC while out celebrating their graduation. Hannah told Mukesh that she was graduating from her University that coming week, and they got to talking more about his travels and cricket. Hannah liked that Mukesh was into sports and told him about her sport of vaulting (gymnastics on horseback).

When Mukesh met Hannah's parents for the first time after a few months of dating, her parents were okay with the idea of her relationship with him. Her parents did not question her decisions growing up, and they took a liking to him. Before they wed, Mukesh met all of Hannah's aunts and uncles on her father's side that lived in the area, and they all loved him.

Hannah ended up meeting Mukesh's mother for the first time a few days before he proposed. Mukesh's mother welcomed Hannah with open arms into the family. Hannah and Mukesh had a wedding in the U.S. and also in India (per Indian customs).

Their Advice For Other Couples

- Respect each other's cultures and upbringing.

- Take time to understand each other's differences.

- Talk about your differences and try to compromise on things that you can. Communication is key. Don't assume your spouse would understand things without sharing that with them.

- Be open to hearing and changing things where needed is essential, and having this flexibility is the key to a great interracial marriage.

- Just remember differences can be worked out no matter where the person is from. You are a team and need to work together for you both to succeed. Be willing to give that extra attention to sort out any little differences that creep in from time to time.

- Learning a new language takes time.

- Do not call your Indian relatives by their name because that is not acceptable in the Indian culture (is what Hannah found out firsthand).

- Always love and respect each other's cultures and beliefs.

Hannah loves the cultural richness that comes with marrying into Indian culture. Not only has she learned to cook tasty Indian dishes, but the clothing is also amazing. Most of all, marrying Mukesh doesn't mean she married just him, she got a new family with their marriage.

Mukesh loved the Christian wedding and was excited for every part of the celebration, including the dancing, receptions, decorations, planning, etc. He also loves American dishes like green bean casserole that Hannah makes. It's the best of both worlds.

Loving You Is Easy

"To love is nothing. To be loved is something. But to love and be loved, that's everything."

~ T. Tolis

Alessandra is Black and Filipino, and she was born and raised in Texas, U.S.A. Her husband, Manish, is Indian, and he was born and raised in Manipal, a South Indian town in Karnataka, India. They are both engineers working on medical devices, and they met at work. Alessandra and Manish slowly became friends and then decided to be in a relationship. Four years later, they were married.

Their Top Advice To Other Couples

- Do not have expectations about anything. Expectations are a recipe for disappointment. The only thing you can do is be present in that moment. Alessandra really admires Manish because he is a carpe diem kind of guy. He does not let one-minute go by where he is not being productive doing something he loves. They literally do not have time for the naysayers. They are way too busy traveling, hiking, biking, or doing other fun things. Looking back, she wishes she had taken situations and people as they were and practiced more equanimity. Naysayers will come around when they see you are happy and passionate about something. If not, keep being present and focus on your life.

- If you are passionate about something – people will notice and get involved. Enthusiasm is contagious, and it makes you want to participate in experiences that your partner is excited about. Manish and Alessandra are both proud of their respective cultures (African American and South Indian). They love doing things together like going to concerts, watching movies, TV, reading, and discussing history books that highlight people of color. The best experience they recently had was going to Trinidad and seeing how their histories merged – seeing how African slaves and Indian indentured servants came to the island and became integrated.

- Figure out what your shared core values are and stick to them. When people ask them, "How do you guys do it – Catholic vs. Hindu? Vegan vs. Meat Eater?" They say it is easy (most of the time). They have shared values that get them through anything.
Respect. Equality. Adventure. Knowledge. Compassion. These are some examples of their values

that help them when they are faced with their personal, or cultural differences. Alessandra and Manish ask themselves how does it fit into their values? They either both criticize and oppose the tradition, are flexible enough to make it into their own or agree to disagree and respect each other's beliefs. They are really excited about their wedding ceremony because they will be picking traditions that are special to them and tailoring them so that they speak to their shared values. Their ultimate advice is to do not just follow tradition; instead, make your own.

We Are One Race

"Color is the only difference. We all belong to one race; we are a part of
the human race."
~ Ashanti & Bhavin

Ashanti is African, and she is from Uganda (East Africa). Her husband Bhavin is Indian, and he is from East India. They met through a mutual friend and have been together for six years after dating for three years.

At first, Ashanti was nervous about meeting Bhavin's parents. She had communicated with them for a year via phone before their marriage. And she did not know how they would react to meeting her physically because they are Indian.

Overall, the meeting was very emotional. Ashanti was showered with love by Bhavin's parents, and she immediately felt at home. When Bhavin first met Ashanti's parents, it was overwhelming because they were dating, but her family liked him instantly.

For Ashanti and Bhavin, it is tough to be in an interracial marriage because it is rare to find Indians marrying Africans. Currently, they reside in Kampala, Uganda with their son. Therefore, people do stare, and it makes them feel uncomfortable at times. Nonetheless, they shrug off the stares and marvel in the beauty of the family they have created together.

Their Advice For Other Families

- Color is the only difference. We all belong to one race; we are a part of the human race.

- Take time to plan for your big day since marriage is supposed to happen once in a lifetime.

- Learn about each other's cultures. Falling in love doesn't need to be from the same culture; different ethnicities can also make love a beautiful thing.

- Today their son is almost two years old, so he will have to learn about their cultural differences as he gets older. They are planning to have him go to school in Africa, and they will gradually teach him about his dad's culture at home. Bhavin speaks to him in his language (Hindi), while Ashanti speaks to him in English.

Long Distance Love

"I hate waiting. But if waiting means being able to be with you, I'll wait for as long as forever to be with you. ~Unknown

When Love Lands

"I carry your heart with me (I carry it in my heart)."

~E.E. Cummings

Adriana is Hispanic. She was born in Puerto Rico and raised in Florida (mainly); then she moved back to Puerto Rico, and finally back to Florida (where they reside). Her husband Madhar is Indian, and he was born and raised in Gujrat, India. They have been happily married and in the same country for 11 years. They were in a long-distance relationship for 8 years before they got married.

Adriana and Madhar met on Yahoo chat when she was a senior in high school (2001). They were close online friends for about 1.5 years, and they would talk online every single day. After 1.5 years, they started liking each other, but they did not know if they would be able to ever meet. Adriana lived in Puerto Rico at the time with her parents, and Madhar lived in India with his parents.

Furthermore, Adriana is Christian, and Madhar is Hindu. Intercultural relationships were not as common as they are today, and they were incredibly young. Adriana's parents are deeply religious, and his parents are too. Therefore, they decided against trying to meet and talked online. They talked almost every day for three additional years.

Adriana told her parents she wanted to meet Madhar and fly to India. They thought she had lost her mind. She was determined to meet him one day, so she ended up getting her passport. He was also trying to meet her, but it had not been possible.

During college, chatting online got a little challenging. Madhar went to college at a tiny remote village with one cyber cafe, and the connection was not all that great. At times, Madhar would write Adriana emails on a word document and go to the cybercafé to paste the text from the word document to an email and send it. If he was in class or had a busy day, his biological brother would paste the word docs to the emails and send it her way. Sometimes, she would buy calling cards and call him via his landlord's phone number. They were both determined to continue communicating daily or almost daily.

After college, Adriana moved back to Florida, and she was on her own for the first time. She got her first job as a teacher. Madhar had started his first job too. Their schedules made it very tricky to talk daily, so they tried to email each other on the days they could not chat. And that is when they both started becoming concerned. How would they keep up with their relationship if their jobs did not allow time for it? They were starting to get anxious about meeting and very restless. It had now been five years of talking online and still not meeting in person.

As a result, Madhar asked Adriana to get her Indian visitor's visa. On the morning of her last day of school/her first-year teaching, she got multiple phone calls from him. Her phone was in the back seat, and she was driving to work. Once she got into her classroom, she called him back, and he asked her: "So are you excited about your summer break?" She said, "yes!" And he told her, you should be because you are coming to India. Adriana thought he was joking, or maybe they would try to plan something and see if it would work out.

Well, he bought the tickets and, at the age of 23, Adriana was going to cross the globe. She was going to travel all by herself to meet a guy she had been talking to online for about five years. Her parents were very anxious, but she had let them know that she needed to do this for herself. They ended up understanding and not making this journey even more terrifying for her.

Finally, after all the wait, they met face-to-face. Adriana was worried, what would happen if there was no chemistry in person, but luckily it felt so real, natural, and right. So much so that Madhar proposed to her the same week, she landed in India, and she said yes.

Madhar and Adriana continued their long-distance

relationship for three years after their first face-to-face meeting. This, of course, means they may have broken the record for the longest long-distance relationship. Adriana would meet Madhar during her summer breaks, and she was able to spend a winter break in India, too.

Truthfully, there were a lot of ups and downs due to family issues. Although Madhar was adopted by his aunt and uncle when he was 2, he still keeps in touch with his biological parents. Hence Adriana has four in-laws because Madhar considers all 4 his parents.

And during Adriana's first trip to India, Madhar lived with his adoptive parents (his aunt and uncle). His adoptive parents did not accept them as a couple. They told her that she could only be his friend and she was very honest with them and told them that he was her boyfriend. She was going to be staying in that house with them for the summer in India, so she wanted to make things clear, and so did he.

However, there was a lot of tension in the air daily. They wanted to enjoy finally being together, but Madhar's adoptive parents were not ok with their relationship. They never treated her badly, but things were very awkward, and she did not feel welcome.

Adriana and Madhar decided to get away and spend a week with his biological parents and to meet his other side of the family. It was literally night and day. His mom saw her, hugged her, and she cried. His dad came home from work, and they immediately got along. Adriana met close cousins, distant cousins, neighbors, and friends. She felt at home. It was beautiful. It was special. They accepted her right away.

After that, Adriana went back to Madhar's adoptive parent's house. Once again, things were not that great. She respects them and all and lived by their rules, but when Madhar held her hand in front of them, things swiftly went south. On her last day in India, she reached out to shake his adoptive dad's hand, and he told her that she was not welcome in that house ever again.

Adriana never saw them again. When they found out that Madhar and Adriana got married years later, they disowned him. They have tried reaching out, unsuccessfully. Adriana wishes things were different. At times there is this feeling of, what did she do wrong? What could she have done differently? She wishes things were simpler, but they are not. Some days she prays that they will be.

Their Advice For Other Couples

- Have a "go-to" phrase as a couple to help get you through the moments when you are being judged as an interracial/intercultural couple. One phrase that helps them "snap out of it" is: "It's about you and me. It is not us and the world." It is their little reminder. You must live that way, if not people's opinions or comments can get to you.

- It is never about one culture taking over another culture. It is about having that unique blend of cultures that very few couples have. You must be tolerant & open-minded most of the time and make sure your partner feels safe, bringing up their perspective on anything and everything.

- Couple's therapy is a good thing! It does not mean that your relationship is ruined or that you have issues. Sometimes couples just need a "tune-up" and need to see things from a different perspective.

- There will always be an adjustment period. No matter how well you think you know the other person when you start living with that person, there will always be a few things that you will disagree with. Give it time, be patient, and always ask if your "opinion" is more important than the love you have found.

- Long-distance relationships are challenging. And intercultural long-distance relationships add one more challenge to the mix. Have trust and faith in each other. Communicate often, and express your concerns when needed, be open. Long-distance relationships are possible, but both sides have to be committed to the relationship. These tips are what got them through their eight year long-distance relationship.

A Long-Distance Marriage

"Having somewhere to go to is home. Having someone to love is family.
And having both is a blessing."
~Unknown

Lydia is African, and she is catholic. She was born in Kenya and raised in South Africa. Her husband, Nikhil, is Indian, and he is Hindu. His family is from Rajasthan, India, but he grew up in South Africa. Currently, Lydia lives in Canada, and Nikhil lives in South Africa, so they have a long-distance marriage. Eventually, Lydia will move back to South Africa.

They met seven years ago at a barbecue in South Africa, and they kept talking because Lydia lost a bet against Nikhil. Since they live in a small city in South Africa, Lydia's mother knew that they were dating Lydia officially told her. Unfortunately, Lydia's dad never met Nikhil because he passed away before she started dating him.

Lydia prepared herself to meet Nikhil's parents but was stressed about everything: her clothes, the gift, etc. However, her nerves quickly calmed because Nikhil's parents welcomed her with an open heart.

Still, they have dealt with cultural biases and judgments

because an Indian person marrying an African person is not common in the world. Additionally, both of their cultures are not very open to marriages with foreigners. Thereby they contend with nasty comments, discrimination, and people saying that the relationship will not last.

For this reason, they put themselves in a bubble at the beginning of their relationship. A bubble with no outside influence to create a solid foundation for their marriage. This way, they could communicate and pray (although they are different religions) about all their challenges.

Their Advice For Other Couples

- Communication is key. They both learned that there is a right and wrong way to say things to each other.

- Be open-minded.

- Stay passionate about learning about each other and new things together.

- Realize an interracial and intercultural marriage of this type is inclusive of the in-laws. The in-laws are an extension of your spouse, and it is not a minuscule part because knowing and understanding your in-laws helps explain who they are as a family/the family dynamics.

- Make sure you completely understand each other's

cultural backgrounds. It is essential before deciding to spend the rest of your life with someone. You have to realize that this is another culture that you will be a part of once you say, "I do."

- No matter what fate sends your way, you must not forget that at the outset, the bond that unites you is love and that bond unites only two people above all else. So, everything is and can be settled if there is love between you two.

Unconventional Love

"Being in an interracial and intercultural marriage in the U.S.A. during such a divisive, and sometimes totally dark time in terms of racial injustices and blatant xenophobia is taxing and illuminating."
~Melissa & Rajesh

Melissa is Caucasian, and she was born and raised in central Pennsylvania. Rajesh is Nepalese, and he was born and raised in Chitwan, Nepal. He moved to the United States as an international undergraduate student.

They met at a nightclub. Melissa had just graduated from college and decided to go on an impromptu beach trip for a weekend with her cousin in the same town where Rajesh happened to be working for the summer. Melissa saw Rajesh at the bar and approached him while getting a drink. They began chatting and spent the rest of the night together. The next day Rajesh invited her for coffee, but she was more interested in hitting the beach. So, she met up with him later that night at another popular party place and they stayed up the entire night talking.

Their dating history is as non-traditional as they are. After first meeting in June 2012, they met up a couple of other weekends that summer. During this time, Melissa was living in Pennsylvania and Rajesh was in Maryland, which is about

5.5 hours away.

Then in the spring of 2013, Melissa joined the Peace Corps and moved to Costa Rica to serve as a volunteer for two years. During her time there, they occasionally kept in touch via social media and Skype. But when Melissa visited Pennsylvania over Christmas, Rajesh came to visit for what was supposed to be only one night. He ended up staying for several days with her and meeting her entire family. On his last night, before Melissa flew back to Costa Rica, Rajesh proposed to try dating exclusively while being long-distance. They ended up doing that for the remainder of her time in Costa Rica. And when her service finished, they decided to get married, after only having a relationship with short visits and many Skype conversations.

Melissa moved in with Rajesh in Maryland (the same place where they had met). Rajesh's parents were not initially supportive of their marriage. Thus, when they first came to the United States, about nine months after they got married, it was disquieting. Frankly, Melissa had no idea how they would treat her. Astonishingly, they were friendly and kind. When she first saw Rajesh's mother, they both teared up as they hugged. There are a lot of language and cultural differences that have been taxing for her to get used to when they visit.

Nevertheless, their second visit, a few months ago, was even better. They speak a few English words, and Melissa is learning a few Nepali words and phrases to help them when they are together. Additionally, having their son has given them something to connect over.

Aside from Rajesh's parents' initial disapproval of the relationship, their obstacles are navigating their different backgrounds, families, and social circles. They both were raised in entirely different cultures and contexts, and these differences sometimes rear their head in their daily lives. For example, Melissa grew up in a conservative, all-white family. And while they are incredibly loving towards Rajesh, they often do not fully understand or appreciate his experience as an immigrant to the U.S.A., and this has been challenging to get across to them.

Furthermore, while as a couple, they tend to have similar spiritual and political beliefs, dietary preferences, and lifestyle, their families are entirely different. Melissa was raised Christian, and Rajesh was raised Hindu. Thereby, it has been challenging to live how they choose to as a couple when it differs a lot from both of their families.

Their Tips For Other Couples

- Be curious, humble, and receptive.

- Since they live in the United States, Melissa must be more mindful that Rajesh's home and culture are elsewhere. Thus, they are creating a life together that includes as much Nepalese culture as they can. Logistically, they just have not been able to travel there together. But they hope to do so soon with their son.

- Try to keep in mind the other's upbringing when you have a difference of opinion. This helps to put everything into context for them.

- It is a cliche, but patience with each other's differences goes a long way in a relationship.

Being in an interracial and intercultural marriage in the U.S.A. during such a divisive and sometimes totally dark time in terms of racial injustices and blatant xenophobia is taxing and illuminating for Melissa and Rajesh. They do not see their relationship as an abstract multicultural perfect image. But instead, as a daily experience that challenges and illuminates their deeply held beliefs and values about the world. And possibly it does the same for others when they see them. Above all, their love is built on their friendship, partnership, and values. Collectively, Melissa and Rajesh believe that this makes all the difference in navigating an interracial and intercultural marriage in today's world.

128

Ready For Love

*"Love someone who leaves so many holes in you that if they were to walk away, half of your soul would go with them." ~*Emery Allen

Justina is Polish, and she was born and raised in Poland. Her husband Ravi is Indian, and he was born and raised in India. They met online in February 2016 via an online dating app. They both logged on, not expecting to find their soulmate, but they did.

At the time, they were both lonely and wanted to see what might happen. Justina had a question on her profile about her favorite tree, and Ravi's first message was just "pine." That evening they wrote to each other for several hours. A couple of days later, they had their first Skype talk because Ravi promised to teach Justina English. Again, they spoke for several hours, and after that day, they continued to talk to each other.

In May 2016, Justina traveled from Poland to India for the first time, and at that time, they knew that we wanted to spend the rest of their lives together. By August 2016, she headed to Delhi, and then Abhi proposed. By the middle of November 2016, Justina moved to Delhi, and on the 10th of December 2016, they were married. They had a small ceremony in the temple.

Presently, Justina and Abhi have been married for seven years. They are fighting for a better life together because they have been a long-distance married couple for the past year, which making things twice as hard. Right now, Justina is living and working in Poland, and Ravi is in India. They would love to live in Poland but have not decided if that is best yet.

Thankfully, they didn't have any problems finding acceptance with their families. Still, interracial/intercultural relationships are tougher. The problem for them is the distance, which they know they will resolve even if it means moving to a different country to be together.

Their Advice For Other Couples

- Everything is about balance. It can't be that you are married to an Indian man, and you are changing into an Indian. Or it shouldn't be. It's like losing yourself. Instead, celebrate each other together.

- Never forget about love. That's why you are together; that's why you have all the strength to fight any problems together.

- Love is the solution, and it is the answer, always!

3. Choosing A Love Marriage After An Arranged Marriage

"Once you stop looking for what you want, you find what you need." ~Unknown

Marrying For Love

"Your dream doesn't have an expiration date. Take a deep breath and

try again."

~ KT Witten

Kevin is Black American, and his wife Maya is Indian. They were both born and raised in the Bay Area, California. They met each other on numerous dating apps and became friends.

Kevin was a bundle of nerves because he thought Maya's parents would not accept him as a Black man. A few Indian people he knew informed him that typically Indian parents are not accepting of their daughters marrying outside of their race or Black men. However, in this case, they were wrong. Maya's parents were beyond welcoming.

Likewise, Maya was greeted with open arms by Kevin's parents at their initial meeting. She was not worried about gaining their acceptance or them not liking her. What's more, she did not openly disclose to them that she had been married before until later. Truthfully, a lot of people did not know that Maya was previously married. Kevin's parents were not too concerned per se, but they did wonder why she was divorced. Once she shared the reason behind her divorce, there were no further conversations.

Throughout their relationship and marriage, Kevin and Maya have dealt with blatant and unexpected discrimination. After Maya started dating Kevin, she had a Black female coworker tell her that she should "leave Black men alone and look for her own kind.' "Black women struggled enough in relationships, and so she should leave their men alone." Maya solely expected this kind of discrimination from her ethnicity/race, so she was quite surprised when she heard this from her colleague.

Kevin and Maya discussed what happened at length, and his family assured Maya that there is nothing wrong with marrying the person you love. Furthermore, perhaps her coworker was projecting her personal insecurities onto her. After that day, Maya did not care much about what anyone thought.

Their Advice For Other Couples

- Love is love. You can't help who you fall in love with.

- When they combined their worlds, they agreed to respect and embrace their cultures. And when they have a family together, they will raise their children to understand both cultures' beauty.

- When you marry each other, your priority should always be the two of you first. Sometimes the going gets tough, and that during those times, support each other culturally and advocate for one another in times of cultural distress.

Kevin and Maya are combining the forces of both their cultures. Maya adores that Kevin tries to learn words in her language, watches Indian movies with her, and hums along to Indian songs when she plays them. Moreover, Kevin partakes in family events and functions as if he were Indian too and vice versa.

Blending Families

"Family *isn't defined only by last names or by blood; it's defined by commitment and by love. It means showing up when they need it most. It means having each other's backs. It means choosing to love each other even on those days when you struggle to like each other. It means never giving up on each other.*"

~Dave Willis

Childhood Friends

"One day, love and friendship met. Love asked, 'Why do you exist when I already exist?' Friendship smiled and said, 'To put a smile where you leave tears."

~ Unknown

Derrick is African American, and Priya is Indian. They grew up next door to each other their whole lives and remained good friends. As kids, they would play outside together; they would playhouse. Their favorite memory together as children is stealing Priya's mom's pots and filling them with dirt and rose petals to make "mud pies." Derrick's parents moved away to a different neighborhood in high school, and they lost touch. In 2010, Priya was outside of her parent's house cleaning her car, and Derrick happened to be driving down her street and stopped to say hi. They exchanged phone numbers, and that is how they reconnected and started dating.

Priya's first meeting with Derrick's parents was a little tricky. Since they grew up next door to each other, his parents knew her, but they did not realize that they were dating. So, when Derrick took Priya over to his parent's home, it was almost normal. They caught up on old times, and they knew she was good for Derrick.

For Derrick, meeting Priya's parents, as her boyfriend, was interesting. Her parents asked for them to all go out to dinner together. Priya was already nervous, so she let them pick the restaurant. They chose an Indian restaurant to dine at, and Derrick almost choked on the Papad. But he made it through the dinner. Priya's parents were nice and asked usual life questions. Derrick started spending more time with her family, coming to a few family gatherings. His first event was Priya's parent's big fourth of July party they did every year. They started to get to know him a little bit better.

After three years of dating, they moved in together, and about a year later, Priya was pregnant. Derrick and Priya were shocked. Their lives were about to change forever. And Priya really did not know how to tell anyone since they weren't married. Priya finally decided to tell her grandmother, who helped raise her, and she was so excited. Priya felt better. But her parents and sister were scared. Priya dating a Black person was already a foreign concept to them because no one in their direct family or friends circle had ever done this. And now Derrick and Priya's two culturally different families had to come together as one. It was not very easy. Their families come from two vastly different backgrounds and upbringings, so naturally, it was challenging to come together as one. Both parents also grew up in different times, where interracial marriage was not common. Hence, Derrick and Priya learned about each other's cultures and even created their own traditions.

Ultimately, once their daughter, Asha, was born, their families had time to get to know each other as a family. Additionally, Derrick has a son from a previous relationship, so they were not only bringing Asha into their lives, but they were also blending their families. Derrick Jr. was eight when Asha was born, and he is honestly the best big brother. Over the years, the two of them have created a strong bond. They both love sports. As a result, their favorite thing to do is to watch Derrick Jr. play football or basketball. And Asha loves it when her brother comes to watch her swim.

For Derrick and Priya, blending the families together has not always been healthy, but their two families have recently created healthy relationships to raise their kids together. They share birthday dinners and attend school games together often. Today, Priya's parents love Derrick, and his parents adore her. Their start was a little rocky. Yet her parents see how much Derrick loves her and takes care of his family, and that is truly all they want. Priya and Derrick are honestly so lucky to have such open-minded families that accept them, and they are grateful for this. While the journey to today was not the easiest – they understand why it was so hard for them. Nonetheless, they wanted to show their families that they are soul mates and are genuinely in love.

Their Advice For Others

- Do what is best for you. Derrick and Priya made a promise to always make each other happy, to focus on what they wanted in life, and to build a life together.

- Be prepared for judgment. Not everyone will understand your relationship, and you must be okay with that.

- Take the time to learn each other's culture, involve them in events, teach them your language, learn with them, and create your own traditions from what you learn.

- Be open-minded and understanding. Derrick and Priya understood why it was so hard for their parents, in the beginning, to accept them. They didn't grow up in a time where it was the norm to be in an interracial/intercultural relationship. Therefore, their job to show them love has no boundaries, no skin color; it is just honest, true love.

- Create your own family traditions that involve both cultures.

Relocating To Another Country For Love

"If we were meant to stay in one place, we'd have roots instead of feet…"

~Rachel Wolchin

Moving To India

"Move out of your comfort zone. You can only grow if you are willing to feel awkward and uncomfortable when you try something new."
~Brian Tracy

Satyam is Indian, and he is from Bihar, India. His wife, Jennifer, is Caucasian-American, and she is from the Midwest U.S.A. Friends introduced them via an organization they volunteered with on different sides of the globe. At the time, Jennifer was posted in India, and Satyam was in the U.S.A. Talk about a geographical flip flop.

They have been together for ten years and married for nine years and have two children. Currently, they live in North India in the state of Bihar. When Jennifer was in her 20's she traveled to India for a business internship and fell in love with India. It was not merely an infatuation with the people and culture instead, she ended up working with wonderful people who became friends, and she felt like India was her second home.

And after meeting Satyam, they conversed about living in India someday. The final decision for their move to India boiled down to their professional and personal skill sets, which are tailored to doing more meaningful and fulfilling work in India than what they were able to do in the U.S.A. for their careers. Hence after living in the America for 6 years, they packed up and moved to India.

At first, moving to India was extremely difficult for Jennifer. She was in her 20's, and like most American women, she highly valued her independence and desired for people to respect her and her opinion. She had to deal with many of the frustrations and struggles that most people go through who move from the West to the East.

It is not the trash or dirt or crowds in India that frustrated her most of the time. It is often the underlying patriarchy, many people's acceptance of mediocrity and obsession with a fatalistic mentality. Those are the frustrations that still keep her up at night, now almost 16 years into engaging with Indian culture.

Advice For Other Couples Considering Moving To India

In short, keep your expectations low. This is as it relates to: your productivity, the culture's ability to deliver what you want, those around you, and most of all, of yourself. Give grace. Lots of it. Practice acceptance of the less than ideal. Practice forgiveness, especially to yourself.

Undeniably, being a foreign wife in India, draws attention; however, they have learned to use it as an asset instead of a liability. How? They utilize their differences to show kindness to people in unique ways rather than get irritated by the extra attention. Also, being notably different races from each other, there have been times when Satyam can get something done because he is Indian, whereas her whiteness wouldn't have the same weight with that person and sometimes vice versa and regardless of whether they are in the U.S.A. or India. It's frustrating that not everyone is treated equally in this world, but it is a reality to have to deal with. And there are, of course, irritations, such as when someone makes a weird comment about one of their kids' appearance or behavior. But for their family, these are manageable, and they don't get easily offended.

Fortunately, when Jennifer and Satyam met each other's parents for the first time, it was pretty laid back. Jennifer's dad met her future in-laws before she did as he had traveled to India and honored Satyam's parents with his visit. While the first time Jennifer met Satyam's parents, she was in India alone on a project and flew to stay with them. In that week, Jennifer went wedding shopping with Satyam's parents, and she bought all her bridal jewelry and sarees.

To the contrary, Satyam met Jennifer's parents down at their lake house. Her parents decided to engage him in all kinds of challenges and tests of his water sports skills. Given that he just learned to swim in his late 20's, he did not impress them with his skills. However, he did impress her with his ability to manage the chaos and go with the flow.

Their Advice For Other Couples

As an Indian/White couple -acknowledge individualism vs. communalism that affects each decision that the other person is making. Western culture is much more centered on making your own choices and feeling empowered to make decisions based on what you want.

In contrast, most Indians are very connected within their family system. They are expected to make life decisions based on the wants and desires of their family. Understanding this will help in accepting the other person and walking through life together with compassion.

Jennifer and Satyam have a sense of belonging to multiple cultures. They both have deeply experienced each other's home culture before they met, so that helps a lot in getting through those problematic cultural adjustment periods like having their first child, changing jobs, the family of origin conflict, or moving countries.

Proving Our Love

"Love is breathing each other with all madness"

~ Seema Gupta

Anaya is Indian, and she was born and raised in Mumbai, India. Her husband, Hyun, is South Korean, and he was born and raised in South Korea. They met while Hyun was working in India and currently live in Korea.

Both parents were warm and friendly during the first meeting. Yet when they told their parents they wanted to get married, at first, they were not happy. Indian society did not readily accept their wedding. They had to work to convince their families to accept each other's cultures and to show them how they could happily conjoin. After doing so, both sets of parents trust and believe in their love, and they agreed to their marriage.

Their Advice For Other Couples

- Interracial and intercultural relationships are complicated, but as long as you both love and support each other, everything else will fall into place.

- Communication is vital for a healthy relationship. Hence be honest with each other and, most importantly, trust each other.

- Interracial and Intercultural relationships are an amazing experience. They enable you to thrive individually and allow you to understand people better. If you are in an intercultural relationship, enjoy every aspect of it because it is such a rare and precious experience.

Finland It Is

"Love is not what you say. It is what you do."

~ Unknown

Jessica is from Finland, and Rahul is from India. They originally met in India in 2011 through a mutual friend and are currently living in Finland. That friend asked Jessica's friend out for a date while they were on holiday/vacation in Goa. Jessica's friend did not feel comfortable going alone, so she joined them. Rahul was there to give her a ride. It was not love at first sight because Jessica thought he was annoying. After some time, their paths crossed again on Facebook, and they started to talk, and they have been going strong ever since.

Their Advice For Other Couples

- Immerse yourself in both cultures/worlds. When there are two different cultures joining in the same household, make the best of it. It is possible and desirable to enjoy both cultures. Think about the things that you both enjoy about each other's backgrounds. Food is a good example here: in the morning, you can indulge yourselves with some idli and sambar or enjoy some oatmeal porridge with blueberries. Open your heart to your partner's culture and try different things. Try to adopt the traditions that are important to your partner.

- Agree to disagree. There are and will be some things in your partner's culture that you may not understand. But that is alright. Learn to agree that sometimes you just disagree about something and respect each other's opinions. After all, if you are raised in different conditions and are from totally different, backgrounds it is not a surprise if your ideologies don't always match. Instead, concentrate on the things you agree on.

United In Love

"I've never had to ask a thing from you, as everything you've ever fed
my soul was love."
~Karen A. Baquiran

Lakshmi is Indian, and she was born in India. Ha-Joon is Korean, and he was born in Korea. They both had never visited a foreign country before turning 20. They met at work in India. Ha-Joon met Lakshmi's entire family. Yet, she did not introduce him as her boyfriend to her parents but instead as a work colleague who was curious about Indian culture. Nonetheless, her mom told her that her dad believed they were dating because she was only hanging out with him. After her father's death, her family became open to their relationship.

On the other hand, Lakshmi has only met Ha-Joon's dad. His mom is not ready to meet her yet. Lakshmi has talked to his brother via texts and hopes to meet him someday soon.

As a couple, Ha-Joon and Lakshmi have confronted and overcome many obstacles. The first issue was language barriers. Neither of them were fluent in each other's native languages. Thereby, they both sought out to learn each other's languages together. The second obstacle was stereotyping and irritating comments from other people. Many of Ha-Joon's colleagues used to ask him if he is sure of the relationship because, in the future, it might not turn out well. In particular, if they have babies, their babies might get bullied in school for being mixed. Additionally, people would continuously tell Lakshmi to be careful because Ha-Joon must just want to sleep with her and nothing else. Although they did not care about other people's opinions, it was not good for their mental health.

As a result, they have this rule of a "crystal clear relationship." They do not keep anything to themselves if someone says something or something bothers them.

The third and last stumbling block they had was accepting their cultural differences. Lakshmi is Indian and Hindu. She does not eat a lot of meat except for Chicken. Beef is something she cannot eat because of her religion, and she refrains from eating meat on Monday, Tuesday, Thursday, or any other religious day. Conversely, Ha-Joon does eat almost all kinds of meat. Therefore, initially, it was tough when they went on dates or traveled, and so Ha-Joon decided to refrain from eating meat when Lakshmi did not. However, today they let each other eat whatever they want. Lakshmi is trying to adapt to eating more Korean food while Ha-Joon loves Indian food.

Their Advice For Other Couples

- Respect and accept each other's cultural differences. Do not try to change them. Those deep-rooted beliefs cannot be changed overnight; it will just make the relationship worse.

- Always be open to each other. Share the things that bother you. Because if you do not and you keep it inside, it can create resentment and anger.

- Try to overcome the language barriers and talk as much as you can. And if you do not understand, just ask your partner to explain it again. Do not ever say yes to things you do not understand.

- Do not force your partner to follow a religion or set of beliefs that are not a part of their culture.

In a nutshell, Lakshmi and Ha-Joon love that their relationship is fun. They came up with their own language code. Also, there is always something new to learn.

Joint Family

"Family, where life begins and love never ends."

~Unknown

High School Love

"Somethings that start in high school last a lifetime."

~Unknown

Beth is a Caucasian woman from the U.S.A. Her husband, Johny, is Indian, and he is from India. They have two precious sons. They lived in the same city but went to different high schools. One day, they met at a local teenage hangout. They talked for a while but forgot to take each other's phone numbers that night. Randomly, Johny's friend asked Beth and her friend to a movie a month later, and luckily Johny came along. They exchanged numbers at that time, and they have never stopped talking.

Beth can never forget the day that she first "met" Johny's mom because it was through email. She lived in India, and he was in the U.S.A. studying abroad. Johny had already told his mom about Beth and she openly accepted her from the first day.

Similarly, Beth's parents approved of Johny after they met him. Thankfully, both of their families were more than accepting of their relationship and love. Still, when Beth found out there was a possibility that her mother-in-law would come live with them, it was a shock. In the early months of her living with them, it was hard. It was a huge cultural shock. At first, Beth did not know how to handle it. She was newly married, pregnant with their first son, and she was not prepared for the changes to come. In India, young girls grow up in a very family-oriented atmosphere. They know they will likely marry into the family of their family's choice. They also know that they will live jointly with their husband's family eventually and take care of their in-laws.

On the other hand, in the USA, the upbringing is different. Traditionally as a child, you do not see your family living jointly; a household consists of a father, mother, and their children. That is what Beth also had in mind before she knew about her mother-in-law coming to live with them permanently.

However, as the days and months passed, Beth learned and adjusted in her own way. The day, Beth and Johny's first son was born is the day her love and compassion profoundly changed, and she felt blessed to have her mother-in-law with them. Rather than a hurdle in their life, she became a huge helping hand. And fast-forwarding to today, they have all been living together for almost five years.

Therefore, Beth matured, adapted, and accepted that this is how life is. She cannot ask for a better family support system. Her mother-in-law is truly one of a kind. She took the role of loving her as her daughter rather than a daughter-in-law. Beth does not call her Sassu or any other mother-in-law term in Gujarati. She is "mom" and that she will always be.

Beth's in-laws may think that they are the lucky ones for Johny choosing her, but honestly, she is the lucky one. They are the best family anyone could ask for in the world. She would hope and wish that every daughter-in-law can grow this type of relationship with their mother-in-law.

Their Advice To Others Living As A Joint Family

- If you can accept each other, you will see the best in each other, and that will lead to you loving each other.

- Before marriage, make sure to discuss topics that may arise a year or so after. Topics such as parents moving in full-time or part-time. This is a huge obstacle many women face that marry an Indian man.

- Both be open, honest, and accepting. Not just one of you, but both.

Their Advice To Other Parents

It is important to celebrate all holidays from both cultures. Do not skip or make one holiday seem less important to your children. Make them feel that both cultures are on the same level of importance, and they will never have to choose which is better.

Transracial Adoption

"Adoption – because family isn't made from blood, it's made from love."

~Unknown

The Beauty Of Adoption

"As a mixed family we loved the thought of mixing it up even more."

~Rebecca & Shaun

Rebecca and Shaun have been married for five and a half years. They have two kids. Rebecca comes from an Indian background, Shaun is Caucasian, Christian is their biological son, and Lilian is their half African American and half Filipino adopted daughter.

When they decided that they wanted to adopt, they very quickly came to the realization that they did not have a preference for race/ethnicity. They felt as a mixed family; they would love to mix it up even more. Also, that they are confident enough in their racial identities to love and empower a child with a different ethnic background than their own.

To prepare for the adoption, they educated themselves before adopting their daughter by taking adoption classes. These classes taught them the importance of empowering adopted children in their racial identities and taught them the common struggles of transracial adoption.

Rebecca's first thought when she saw her daughter for the first time is that "she's absolutely beautiful!" Lillian was born with the biggest, fluffiest cheeks. She still has them. She was such a dreamy infant, and still is quite the charmer. For Rebecca it was a bit hard to believe that everything would go okay, that all the paperwork would get signed, and that Lillian would come home with them. Yet she has and they couldn't feel more complete as a family.

What's more, Lillian is blessed to have the kindest birth mother. She loves Lillian and has always wanted her to have a loving home. Rebecca and Shaun are incredibly blessed to have a great relationship with Lillian's birth mom. So far the biggest learning curve, with the adoption has been learning to take care of curly hair. She has a combination of African American and Asian hair. At first, Rebecca would just brush it and put bows and headbands in it. Over time, she realized that she needed to learn how to define and maintain her beautiful curly hair. She is now in Facebook groups that are specifically for transracial adoptive families that need hair tips.

Interestingly enough, as a family they have not gotten any rude comments, but maybe that is because Lillian is only ten months old. They do, however, get looks, especially if Shaun is holding Lillian. He has been stared at, looked up and down. People may wonder if he is kidnapping a baby, or honestly, some people probably think Rebecca had Lillian with a different "baby daddy." Regardless, Shaun and Rebecca don't really care what people think, and if people ask, they love telling them about the beauty of adoption.

When it comes to educating Lillian about her rich cultural background, Shaun, and Rebecca plan to read books, go to museums, cultural events, and festivals, in addition to enjoying different cultural food. They feel blessed to have Filipino and African American friends who can speak into Lillian's life, and at the same time, educate them.

Their Advice For Others Considering Adopting

For those interested in adopting, they would suggest that you make room in your heart. If your heart is open to loving a child who doesn't look like you, then get ready because they will completely win you over!

From IVF To Adoption

"Maybe these are meant to be our babies..."

~Erica & Craig

Erica is a stay-at-home mom who works harder than she ever did in the private sector but, that's just parenthood. She is married to a great man named Craig who also happens to be a pediatrician. As it turns out, they ended up really needing his physician connections. They have a son, who was born with an exceedingly rare kidney condition. He is strong, confident, and keeping him healthy is a full-time job. When he was a baby, they could not imagine having more children.

Erica could not see past the day to day struggles of keeping him healthy. As the years went by and the hospitalizations started happening less frequently, they started daydreaming of more children. Additionally, Erica had a difficult pregnancy, and they knew there was a chance that it could happen again. Therefore, Erica and Craig consulted with a fertility specialist to see what their options were. IVF was a possibility but could not guarantee a smooth pregnancy. They wanted to expand their family, so they decided to give it a try. Insurance denied coverage of the IVF. Thus, they appealed and waited for their response.

One night, while Erica was with some mom friends, one

mom, Stacy, shared a story of a birth mom who had contacted her about finding a family for her unborn twins. Stacy is a surrogacy attorney and does not handle adoptions, but something about the story resonated with Erica. She shared the story at dinner on Nov 3, 2016. Erica said, "Stacy, maybe these are meant to be my babies," and she texted Craig, right then and there, "do you want to adopt 28-week-old twins"? To which he promptly replied, "sure." The table had a good laugh, and that subject was dropped.

The next morning, Erica and Craig received two messages. 1st, insurance approved their first set of IVF tests, and 2nd was a text from Stacy that read, "I don't know if you were serious last night but, I contacted the birth mom, and she would like to speak with you, are you available in 30 minutes?". On November 4, 2016, they responded to only one of those two messages, and, 30 minutes later Erica was speaking to Elizabeth, their daughter's birth mom.

On Nov 7, 2016, they met Elizabeth in person, and on Nov 9, 2016, they entered a contract through an open adoption agency. On Nov 10, 2016, they met with their daughters' birth father, and two months later on, Jan 12th, 2017, they welcomed their daughters into this world. Erica held Elizabeth's head in the delivery room while she pushed. It was truly a miracle to be present for the birth of their daughters. And an honor to cut both umbilical cords, transitioning their daughters from the woman who gave them life to the woman who would teach them how to live, learn, and love.

Overall, the open adoption process Erica and Craig went through required them to answer many questions around their comfort level with transracial adoption. Because Erica is biracial, she did not think twice about entering a transracial adoption. She grew up with a Black dad and a Caucasian/Jewish Mom. So, learning that their racial background was an Indian birth father and Caucasian birth mother seemed like a perfect match to them. They are a biracial family; Erica is mixed, and Craig is Caucasian. They are already raising a multiracial child. Again, the pieces just seemed to fit, and they started to educate themselves.

The first time Erica and Craig first saw and held their twins in their arms they thought, "a miracle happened, they are beautiful, God's plan had worked", and on January 12th, 2017, they went from a family of 3 to a family of 5.

Since their daughters are Indian, and White, Erica and Craig talked extensively about how to honor their daughters' Indian culture, and to expose them to "people who looked like them". They reached out to their friends and started to build a community of Indian contacts they could call on. They read books and watched programs, and learned about the different Indian holidays, and talked about which ones they wanted to incorporate into their family. After their girls were born, social media became a huge support for Erica. Presently, she has made friends across the globe who have been a huge source of guidance and information.

Their Advice For Other Couples

- Be honest with yourself about what it means to raise a child from a different culture than your own.

- Love is important, but it is not the only thing a child needs.

- We all want to belong or fit somewhere; make sure you are open and able to create a space where your child can feel like they "fit" socially, culturally, and emotionally.

Love Beyond Gender

"Love has no age, no limit; and no death."

~John Galsworthy

Radical Curls and Red Curry

"You May Never Know What Result Of Your Action. But If You Do Nothing There Will Be No Result."
~ Mahatma Gandhi

Rajika is South Indian, and Monica is African American. Rajika was born and raised in Maryland. Monica was born and raised in Missouri. They met in N.Y., USA, on a Bumble dating app, so it was "like at first swipe!" Their "first sight" was really to make sure that the other person was real. They were both looking for a summer fling at the time. But they were immediately struck by how easy it was to talk to each other. Rajika is a musician. Therefore, their first date was to grab a quick dinner on a random waterfront between Monica's workday and before Rajika's rehearsal. Monica made reservations so Rajika would not be late to her rehearsal, and Rajika brought her violin with her.

It was also Rajika's first time going on a date with a woman. Consequently, the date started humorously with the hosts and waiters calling Rajika "Monica" until Monica arrived. Even though time was limited, their short date turned into a long and winding walk as Monica decided to drop Rajika off at rehearsal. They talked about family, culture, their journeys towards queerness, art, politics, food, and more!

Rajika grew up in a family where queerness was always discussed as an option. That open-heartedness lent itself well to seeing herself as being able to love any gender. Because she was very feminine while growing up, though, she struggled to see how she would fit into a queer relationship and what that would look like. There is a way that your gender conditioning can dissuade you from witnessing your sexuality.

For Rajika, it often felt like her femininity was for the male gaze. As a result, she did not quite know how to place her attraction to women. After meeting Monica, she was able to understand that her femininity could coexist with her queerness. And this time, it was a radical choice to lean into her femininity for *herself* and not for anyone else. Since she grew up always being an advocate and "ally" for the LGBTQ+ community, whenever someone said, "When you have a husband," she would interrupt with "or wife!" Now, she and her family can understand that that passion was rooted in her *own* queerness. And it has been easy to see how much more vibrant, creative, and open she is when her queerness is fully expressed.

On the contrary, Monica had been interested in and dated women for about ten years. However, sharing this with both family and friends was a slow process. She had a "fling" with her college roommate, and everyone knew they were awfully close. However, it was not something that was discussed. Monica grew up in a Catholic household and attended Catholic school for twelve years. And in the eyes of the church, marriage between a man and a woman is a sacrament and preserving their definition of the family unit is crucial.

Being queer was just something Monica never thought about seriously until her twenties. And by her late twenties, her family probably had more of an inkling since Monica never talked about guys or ever introduced them to anyone. It was not until last April, right before she turned 31, that she verbally shared with her mom that she was dating a woman. This was a woman Monica was dating for a few months before meeting Rajika. She casually mentioned it to her mom as she was saying goodbye to her at the airport before she boarded a plane back to New York. Monica's mom was more surprised that she was dating anyone, let alone a woman! She was just so happy that Monica was happy. It was a freeing feeling to finally have relief from the pain of hiding for so many years.

Monica had never brought home a partner to meet her parents and was not intending on it anytime soon. Last November, however, Monica's darling dog Roo got extremely sick. Rajika offered to join their drive to Missouri for

Thanksgiving. It was Rajika's first time meeting a partner's parents, and the whole thing caught Monica by surprise. But because they were all so invested in Roo's health, it felt like they were already family. The need to come together pushed the nerves aside and formed a space for them to build a quick and meaningful bond. The whole visit brought Monica closer to her family too.

Because Rajika comes from a family of musicians, her father and sister were always around at performances, etc., from the beginning of their relationship. The more significant step for them was when Rajika took Monica to India this past summer to meet her 94-year-old paternal grandmother, Thathi! It was Monica's first trip so far outside the U.S.A, and Thathi does not speak English. Thathi had asked Rajika to bring Monica to her so that she could "check out her character," which she could only do in-person

Between the lengthy travel, the language barrier, the new culture, and wanting to make a good impression without being able to communicate verbally, Monica was incredibly nervous. She was also worried about the cultural and generational implications and how Thathi felt about queerness in general. She quickly realized that she and Thathi did not need verbal communication to connect and understand the love they mutually shared for Rajika; akin, to their love of the Hindu god Ganesha, and mangos obsessively wiping down countertops, and so much more. Within a few minutes of meeting Monica, Thathi said, "Nalla Jodi! A perfect match. Yenakku thrupthi! I'm satisfied." After ten days together, Monica walked away feeling like she had gained a grandmother in Thathi. It was special to have an elder bless their queer and interracial relationship.

Often because they are in a queer relationship, they do not rely on cultural blueprints for what a romantic relationship or marriage is supposed to look like. They are both incredibly grateful for this because it presents them with an opportunity to create a blueprint that is entirely theirs. They are not dependent on any predominant culture of gender roles, family structure, etc.

That said, they do come across cultural differences around communication, individualistic vs. collective decision making, financial decisions and insecurities, work ethic, and more.

Their Advice For Others

- Queerness and mental health awareness are an asset (for them).
- When something comes up, take a step back. Observe your histories (personally, culturally, and spiritually)

when trying to communicate with one another. This allows you to separate yourself from the personal and intergenerational trauma.

- Observe your relationship as a space for healing generations of colonization, enslavement, patriarchy, homophobia, etc.

Remarrying Each Each
Remarrying Each Other After Divorce

"Your dream doesn't have an expiration date. Take a deep breath and try again."

~KT Witten

Redeeming Love-Why We Got Married, Divorced, and Married Again

"Never marry the one you can live with, marry the one you can't live without."

~ James C. Dobson

Heather is Caucasian, and her husband, Jitesh, is Indian. They consider themselves to be an improbable couple. Heather was born in Nebraska, but her family is from Kentucky. Her family is of English, Irish, and Scottish descent. Jitesh is of Gujarati Indian descent. He was born and raised in a segregated South Asian community named Lenasia in Apartheid, South Africa.

Heather and Jitesh were married for 24 years before they divorced and remarried each other two years later. In total, they have known each other for 31 years, and they have five children together. They met in 1988, when Heather was 16 years old, working a night shift at a Baskin Robbins near her home. Jitesh walked in to borrow drink cups for the Baskin Robbins his parents owned. Heather fell in love at first sight of his exotic looks, jet black hair, warm dark brown eyes. He was so different from any boys she knew. Jitesh, however, loves to point out to the world that it was not love at first sight for him. He even relished sharing it on a BBC program interview they were on. And Heather imagined shooting daggers at him with her eyes that day across the microphones. Nevertheless, they were inseparable from their first date.

While dating, they hung out with Jitesh's buddies and brother a lot. And they stayed far away from his parents and the Gujarati community. He was a handsome young man on track to be a doctor. Having an arranged marriage was the expectation, and her sudden presence on the scene threw a wrench in his family's plan for him.

Consequently, the first time she met his parents, she panicked, and she was thrilled at the same time. His mother had her over for a dinner of vegetable biryani, was very warm and friendly, but boy was Heather taken aback when they both ate with their fingers. This was her first step toward falling into the rabbit hole of Indian culture. She met his father shortly after, who was also very welcoming but Jitesh and Heather felt his parents were just playing nice. What they really wanted was for Jitesh to break up with her and go the arranged marriage route because it was what they knew and had always wanted for him.

Jitesh and Heather married for the first time in 1992. She is quite sure that they are in small company with other couples regarding their weddings because they have had three.

Their first and legal wedding was by a judge, attended by immediate family members only and casual. She still cracks up today that his uncles wore tracksuits to the event. He needed instant green card status for student loan eligibility before they could plan an elaborate wedding, so that is why they did this.

Six months later, they had a big Christian wedding in a church, attended by over two hundred of his family and friends, and roughly fifty of hers. They had a buffet of Indian food straight from the kitchens of Gujarati family and friends, and his parents presented Heather with a traditional gift of a sari and jewelry. She had always teased Jitesh about how uncomfortable he was showing public affection for her around Indians, so on their first dance to an INXS song, she held him close to her the whole time, while he laughed, stiff muscled, and embarrassed about his Ba (grandmother) seeing them so close. His mother did not ask them to have an Indian ceremony, which at the time upset Heather, because she received that as a message of their disapproval of their union. They had a rocky start all around, and after five children, and 24 years of ups and downs of joyful times with their family, and angering times of cultural clashes in their marriage, and child-rearing, they divorced.

So many factors went into causing the divorce, like

clashes with one another about family boundaries. His parents expected to walk into their house unannounced and have a strong role in their daily lives. On the other hand, Heather expected to have the American separateness of house and home like she was raised with. His mother and Heather staged tugs-of-war for his loyalty with food, standing over him, testing him, daring him to eat the other woman's cooking.

The foundation of their marital problems was the result of the fundamental differences in the definition of marriage they were raised with as children. Heather was brought up by parents who fell in love and eloped, who had an affectionate marriage based on their love, independent of her grandparents. He was raised by parents who had not met until their wedding. And they had a marriage of obligation to family, children, and the community. Heather wanted a marriage where a man cleaves to his wife, as the Bible declares, and he did not understand how to make that happen.

The warning signs boiled for years as they grew apart. Heather's focus was on parenting, and he was concentrating on his career. Inevitably, they just stopped caring about what the other felt. They were always best friends but lost the love connection in the mix. They decided to divorce but keep their friendship and share their deep devotion to their children.

While divorced, they both had time to learn who they are as individuals. Heather did some online dating, determined to find a western man who would put her first, and which resulted in some hilarious and ludicrous scenarios. Dating in your forties is a train wreck and should be avoided if you can. She also taught ESL full time and became a different person. Jitesh could breathe away from the stress of Heather and from his family and became a different person, too. Jitesh and Heather remained connected because of their children.

After she ended a relationship with someone six months after their divorce, Jitesh and Heather rekindled their friendship, and then their love. She appreciated how Jitesh still looked out for her, how she still cared about his well-being, and how they recognized changes in each other revolve around some extraordinarily crazy circumstances.

So, they dated in secret for a while because they finally recognized the need for private space to redevelop their relationship. Over long night phone calls and dates over sushi and drinks, they picked up the pieces of what they loved in their lives together. Together they redefined what culture meant in their family and left the rest behind. Jitesh and Heather remarried each other two years after their divorce. They went to the local county courthouse and took their children out for a hibachi dinner afterward. Remarriage completed the circle to unite their family once and for all.

As a result of getting divorced and remarried to each other they learned that they are separate people who need space to do their own thing. Also, that when compromise results in one spouse feeling cheated or unheard, it is not a compromise. Heather learned that as a woman, she has the right to use her voice, to be heard, and to permit herself to find joy outside of her marriage and children. And that marriage is a life journey that does not come with a handbook for either spouse. Finally, they learned to show the best and the worst of themselves to each other and not to expect perfection in anyone.

Heather and Jitesh have thirty-one years of stories and obstacles. Most symbolic was when, early in their marriage, Jitesh's relatives sat her at the children's table for family meals, because she was not a man and could not be with him, but she wasn't really one of the women, and couldn't be with them. Her race sort of exiled her from the family structure, and she begged him to stand up for her. Eventually, he did keep her by his side, and they distanced themselves from the Indian community, which was painful for him. Heather's family welcomed him with open arms but did not understand his family's way of doing things, so that was awkward.

Nonetheless, as they all got older and wiser, they all grew to see, they are family, and that is all that matters. Heather's father-in-law and late dad became good friends, and her mom and mother-in-law shop together all the time now.

Their Advice For Other Multicultural Families

- First and foremost, begin talking with your children immediately about race, culture, and family. Children learn who they are by watching their parents and asking questions. In all things, whether it be about why mommy is white and daddy is brown or where do babies come from, honesty and openness are essential for children's well-being and identity. When interracial and intercultural children are secure at home, they are equipped to handle dialogue about their background in the outside world.

- Teach and show your children that each side of the family is valuable and equal. Their son's friend once told him his paternal grandmother was not going to heaven because she was not Christian. Boy, that infuriated them. But he was repeating the lessons from beliefs he was being taught at home; to each his own.

- Teach your children about both religions and cultures

and love their grandparents in that fullness. They will decide how to live their own lives as adults with all the love you have equipped them with.

- Find your tribe to confide in and share support with. They did not know anyone else in their kind of marriage and family for years, and it was lonely. Yet now they have connected with people like them. It makes a world of difference.

What Is Your Story

Personal Narratives

"Stories are the communal currency of humanity."

~Tahir Shah

Too Black To Be Indian But I'm Both

"I remember one of the Indian guys asking my dad in front of me,

"Who is this little Black boy that's with you?" ~ Harrison

Harrison is Black and Indian/South Asian. His mother is Black, of African descent by way of the Caribbean. She was born in St. Kitts, U.S.V.I. She left her island at 17-yrs-old and traveled to St. Thomas, U.S.V.I., and eventually to the U.S.A. His father is Indian. He was born and raised in the largest city in the country of India called Mumbai. His mother is Christian, and although he does have Hindu relatives, his father's immediate family is also Christian.

Harrison's mother became a Christian missionary at a young age and an evangelist. She began traveling extensively and preaching in many different countries. One summer, her faith took her to Mumbai, India. While in India, she was stationed at a church that happened to be his father's family church. Harrison's parents met that summer and started to fall for each other. His father began to court, his mother. By the end of that summer, Harrison's father had asked his mother to marry him.

Confronting Racism From Both Sides Of His Family

Back in the U.S.A., Harrison's parents dealt with racism from both sides. Black people were not able to figure out why his mom was with his dad, and Indian people questioned why his dad was with his mom. His parents credit their faith in God for overcoming all those challenges.

Since he was a child, Harrison knew he was mixed. However, he did not understand how different he was until he saw how his dad was treated around other ethnicities and the same thing with his mom. He also realized that he did not look like what the standard of a mixed-raced kid should look like /appear.

Identifying As Black

For this reason, growing up, Harrison identified more with his Black side. He does not know if it is because his father did not have any family in this country, or he did not look like what the standard of a mixed kid should look like in America. Also, most often, he was around the Black side of his family, so that is what he identified with at the time.

Furthermore, there was an occasion when Harrison happened to be with his dad while he was meeting up with some of his Indian friends. Harrison remembers one of the Indian guys asking his dad in front of him, "Who is this little

Black boy that's with you?" Knowing that his differences were amplified did not feel too good.

Celebrating Being Black And South Asian

Nevertheless, today Harrison celebrates both of his cultures. He acknowledges traditions and holidays that are prominent throughout Indian and African cultures.

Harrison's Advice To Multiracial/Multicultural Kids

- Be patient.

- You will find yourself. Do not overly try and sometimes stereo-typically try to be whatever ethnicity you feel you are lacking.

- You don't have to try and fit in a box. Be proud to create a new box.

Harrison's Advice To Parents

Do not draw the line between the ethnicities. Allow your family to organically and authentically embrace as much of each culture without forcing anything. Sadly, many people are culturally insensitive to the unique struggles of biracial people.

What Harrison Wishes Others Knew

It might take your kids a while to figure out the best way for them to wear their hair (LOL). In all seriousness, don't conclude or judge that a person's decorum is inauthentic based on how they look.

Yes, I Am Latina And I Am Desi

"The biggest struggle that I've faced is that people have repeatedly told me that I am not enough. In the Desi community, I have been constantly reminded that I am "the mixed" child." ~Nadia

Nadia is Salvadorian, Puerto Rican, and Pakistani. Her mother is Salvadorian and Puerto Rican, and her father is Pakistani. Naida has always known that she was multiracial. At a young age, she spoke Spanish at home with her mom, nanny, and her maternal grandparents when they visited. Also, during that time, her paternal grandparents lived with them, so she heard Urdu all the time. Nadia thought it was normal to be in a household with so many languages happening all at once.

On top of that, Nadia went to a Muslim school that was diverse. She heard all kinds of languages throughout the day. So being around different languages and cultures all at once felt like home.

Never Feeling Desi Enough

Growing up, the biggest struggle that Nadia has faced is that people have told her repeatedly that she is not enough. According to each culture (Pakistani and Latina), she is bits and pieces of each of them. In the Desi community, she has been constantly reminded that she is "the mixed child." From her curly hair and appearance to not being able to speak Urdu, that made her different from everyone. She has never felt whole from her pre-teens onward because of the Desi community, making her feel like being a Latina is wrong or that she was too Americanized. That is why she embraced her Latina side so much over the years because that side did not have many issues with her being part Desi.

Currently, she still struggles with her Desi side because she is not really a part of the Muslim community anymore. She does have Desi friends, and they are incredible people, but she still has this weird feeling of not being Desi enough. She feels Latina enough; it's just the Muslim/ Desi side that she still feels so out of place with.

Celebrating Both Cultures But Leaning Latina

Today, Nadia lives in Los Angeles, and the Latinx community is huge there, and it has always been more comfortable for her to connect to that side of herself. Additionally, she spends a lot of time with her mom, and they jam hard to Mana together and go to her Tia's (Aunt's) house to watch novellas and make pupusas and champurrado.

Even though Nadia leans more Latina, she cherishes

both of her cultures. She celebrates being Desi and Latina by eating the food from both of her cultures, learning the history, the music, watching Bollywood movies (a guilty pleasure), keeping up with pop culture and news.

Nadia's Advice For Other Multiracial/Multicultural Kids

- Understand how beautiful you are. The splendid blend of the cultures you represent, however many it may be. You have a special place here in this world.

- It is okay not to know or to be proficient at all of your familial languages.

- You can embrace your cultures in any form that you want to and do it in your own way.

Nadia's Advice For Parents

- Read stories and folklore to your children from your own country or your childhood. Continuously show them how unique and beautiful their cultural backgrounds are.

- Remind them every day that they are the perfect blend of everything.

- Make your child aware that people will say hurtful things but not to let those hurtful things affect them and to stay strong.

- Let your children know it is alright to speak up when someone says something about where they come from, even if it is a family member.

- Most of all, let your children know that it is acceptable to make their own blend of who they want to be. They are enough!

My Search For Identity After Being Abandoned By My Indian Family

"My father's parents threatened to commit suicide if, after coming to the U.S.A., he married a woman who was not a high caste Indian or their choosing."

~ Saraswati

Saraswati is her mother's only child. Her mom is African American, and she grew up in Detroit, MI. Saraswati's father was from India and grew up in Mumbai; her parents met while they were both studying at Michigan State University. Her mother was an undergraduate student focusing on urban planning, and her father was an international graduate student from India working on a Ph.D. in chemistry. At the time, Saraswati's mom had an interest in photography. She thought her father was striking and asked to take his photo.

An Unwelcomed Relationship

However, Saraswati's parents' relationship was not welcome even though her father's parents were in India this whole time. Instead, they threatened to commit suicide if, after coming to the U.S.A., he married a woman who was not a high caste Indian of their choosing. Whether they learned that her parents were married or that she existed is something that she does not know. Yet, she also does not get the impression that they would have been too fond of the idea because her father abandoned them when she was a baby. He left, and Saraswati never again saw the man whose mother's name and whose first name she would carry through life. With few job opportunities in Detroit, Saraswati and her mom moved to New York City when was five years old. She grew up in Queens, NY.

I'm Black And South Asian

Saraswati realized early on that she was biracial. Her Black family members and plenty of other people in her community tended to make a whole lot of comments about her hair. In particular, that it grew long, that she had "Indian" hair and all of that. It was one of the essential ways that she was constantly reminded of being mixed and other. Saraswati was never really around South Asians until she got to the sixth grade and started attending a diverse elementary school in Queens. She was always aware that her name is Indian and that there were aspects of her physical appearance that people thought made her "Indian." Other than that, she knew next to nothing about South Asian cultures and identity growing up.

Facing Discrimination

This lent to Saraswati having a complicated matrix of prejudice and discrimination coming from many different angles. Her Indian family abandoned her. That rejection was her first introduction to prejudice and discrimination. As a child, she was bullied by kids in her neighborhood who resented the attention she got for having long hair. They did not think she was Black enough or they hated her for being different. When she attended mixed schools in Queens, she would get harassment from white students who made a sport out of taunting Indian kids by putting on stupid "Apu" accents (from the Simpsons) and making jokes about red dots and curry. Fighting off anti-Blackness in the U.S.A., and across the world is an on-going struggle.

For this reason, Saraswati still struggles with the anti-Black biases that are all too prevalent in the South Asian community. It is enraging and frustrating. Things have gotten a bit better. She has met a lot more mixed South Asian and Black families. There are still way too many bigots among South Asian grandparents, aunties, and uncles. But it is nice to see more mixed kids (and not just the ones who are mixed with white) being accepted. That gives her more hope for her place in the community. Despite the racism part, she has long felt a compelling connection to the cultural aspects of her ancestry - the food, music, dance, art, celebrations, literature, philosophy, spiritual principles, and visual beauty of South Asian heritage speak to her soul.

Visiting India For The First Time

Saraswati finally visited India for the first time in 2017, at the age of 40. It took her a long time to get around to this trip. Honestly, for many years, she deliberately avoided India because it felt too emotionally loaded of a journey. She was afraid of feeling even more rejected. Much to her surprise, she loved being in India. She stayed in the south and spent the greater part of her time in Tamil Nadu and Kerala. Of course, there were challenges and concerns. India is India. But overall, she felt incredibly at home, welcome, and warmed by the whole experience. The connection to something deep inside of her being that was long neglected felt genuinely profound. Also, it was revelatory to see dark-skinned South Indians going around looking about as Black as Black can be. Saraswati could recognize the anti-Blackness she experienced from Indians as part of deeply ingrained self-hatred, colonization, and caste discrimination. She went back to India this past February, and she plans to continue visiting South Asia in the future.

Celebrating Being Black And South Asian

Today, Saraswati feels that it is her responsibility to celebrate her origins. Embracing her Indian-ness is an act of resistance and self-actualization because ignorance and bigotry conspired to try to deny her of this part of her origins. Embracing her Blackness is an act of resistance and self-actualization because bias against Black people is systemic and global. Choosing self-love is a powerful antidote.

When she got married last year, it was not a traditional or formal ceremony, but she wore a sari for the first time in her life. It felt important to her. She tries to honor her African and slave ancestors by engaging in human rights advocacy and fighting against racism. She has been involved in political activism in some form or another since she was a teenager.

Saraswati's Advice To Other Children and Parents

Abandonment and rejection are a heavy burden to bear. She knows that it has impacted her in profound ways. At times, she found herself in lonely and dark places where she doubted her very right to exist. There is a lot of pain that she negotiates. It does not go away. For those of you who carry family rejection due to racism and bigotry, it can feel like a whole culture and history has denied you.

Saraswati's advice is to keep in mind that the people

who cause you pain are just scratches on the surface. Your connection to who you are and where you come from runs much deeper than them. The kids who attacked her when she was a child caused her trauma, but they are not the gatekeepers to her Blackness. She gets to be as Black as she wants to be. It is her birthright to bask in the beauty, talent, and magnificent legacy that are part of the Black experience.

Likewise, her Indian family does not get to decide if she is welcome in her own origins story. Nope, sorry, but she still gets to be as South Asian as she wants to be. With more than a billion people of Indian origin and tons of languages and cultural diversity all across the diaspora, inevitably, there must be a place for her. Mixed folks are blessed with a rich background that leaps beyond boundaries. They are gifted with a unique perspective on the world.

What Saraswati Wishes Other Knew

Therefore, embrace all the parts of your origins without reducing the value of any of them. Identity is not zero-sum. If you are cooking Indian food or trying to learn Tamil, this does not mean Team Black lost out today. If you are up in your Black family reunion doing the electric slide on the dance floor, it doesn't mean you shut the door on being Desi. "Some of us are more than one box. Some of us are even "all of the above." Very few people have a 100% pure 23 and me report. Perhaps learning to appreciate biracial people can teach everyone to become more enriched by their own complexities.

Yes, I'm Biracial, But I Embrace Being African American

"What do I say when people ask me what's my ethnicity?" ~ Felicity

Felicity is Black and Filipino. Her father is Black, and her mother is Filipino. As a child, she recalls asking her dad, "what do I say when people ask me what's my ethnicity". His response was to tell people that she is Black, and he proceeded to explain a concept that she will now refer to as the "one drop rule." She left that conversation even more confused, but she is glad they had it.

Felicity recollects another conversation with her Aunt (on her dad's side). Her aunt told Felicity that she was bullied as a kid because her friends didn't believe that she or her grandmother (Felicity's aunt's mom) were Black. Felicity's grandmother abruptly showed her aunt her birth certificate which had Black as her race on it for extra reassurance.

Even though the conversations Felicity had with her family as a young girl didn't point her in any direction in terms of how she identified herself, the comical and sometimes confusing experiences have stayed with her after decades just because the conversation took place.

I'm Black

Felicity came to identify herself as Black as a result of a few specific experiences and people in her life. Her aunt (on her dad's side) is her inspiration, and she has always presented herself as a strong, smart, successful Black woman who played a huge role in her South Side Chicago community. Felicity wanted to be just like her as a kid and still strives to live up to her legacy.

Middle school was hard for Felicity as it relates to fitting in. She did not have any Black friends because she was in different classes, and they would make fun of her because she "talked white." However, once she went to college, and she found herself struggling in her classes, Felicity was able to bond with a small group of Black engineers. They always looked out for each other and grew their small community to help push them through the rigors of their curriculum. It was the first time Felicity felt like she was a part of something, and when they had time, they would give back and encourage other aspiring minorities to major in science-related fields.

Felicity's Advice For Others

Many people have this theory that mixed kids have an identity crisis, but Felicity's personal belief is that it is not entirely true. She has always known what she identifies as at an early age, but she became confused because of societies perception of her. Having straight hair, fair skin, and talking "white"/being intelligent has always caused her to be labeled as something other than Black.

For this reason, Felicity believes the biggest thing that parents can do for their kids is the following.

- Let your kids decide for themselves what they identify with (don't have expectations).

- Teach your kids to be confident in themselves, so they can be proud and stand up to anybody and in any situation.

- Expose your children to both cultures (although important) comes after confidence and self-love.

I'm Afro Indian And A Transgender Woman

"My parents and grandparents put me in conversion therapy, hoping it would fix me. And they clearly wasted their money." ~ Alana

Alana is Afro Indian Caribbean and a first-generation American. She was born and raised in NYC and Florida. She moved to Florida when she was thirteen years old, and she is the oldest of seven children. Her parents remarried after her birth, so she is the only child between them. Her mom is Jamaican and Punjabi. Her maternal grandmother is a biracial (Black and White) Jamaican from Clarendon, and her maternal grandfather is from Chandigarh, India. Alana's mom is the youngest of 4 children who were all raised in Jamaica.

On the other hand, Alana's father was born and raised in Chiguanas, Trinidad. Her paternal grandmother is an Afro Trinidadian from Trinidad, and her paternal grandfather is from Surat in Gujarat, India. Her father is the youngest son of 4 children.

Being Multiracial And Transgender

Growing, Alana did not realize her color or ethnicity because they were all the same. Yet when she moved to Florida as a teenager, things were starkly different. She was one of three Black people in her entire high school and one of two Indians in the high school. The other Indian student happened to be the valedictorian that year, but she was a freshman, and Alana was a senior, so they never connected.

Therefore, while Alana was in high school, she felt forced to adhere to an African American identity. Alana wasn't allowed to express herself as an Afro Indian Caribbean or a mixed person. Her high school years were surrounded by people who looked nothing like her. Everyone was White, East / South East Asian, Latino, or African American. And the mixed kids that attended her school were either Black and White or White and Asian. No one had the experience as a Caribbean person or was Black and Asian.

Moreover, at that time, the beauty standard was Paris Hilton, and all the popular girls had blue eyes and blonde hair. They had Tiffany tennis bracelets and charms. Their boyfriends were cute "all American" athletes. Alana wanted to be them and have that, but she was constantly reminded that she was not that, and so she could not have those things. Being transgender was an added layer as she lived in secret until she was seventeen.

However, when she transitioned, she was the only openly trans person in the county. They didn't have LGBTQ Centers, pride, or a community presence. She started the first Gay, straight alliance at her college, but she was the only trans person in these spaces. And so, she looked to cis women for guidance to her journey into womanhood.

When Alana Knew She Was Transgender

Alana knew she was transgender when she was three years old. Alana and her aunt were playing house and she told her aunt that she was a girl. Alana does not have a recollection of the conversation. However, when she was eighteen and a year into her transition, she was on the phone with her aunt wishing her a happy birthday, and she reminded Alana of that story, and it aligned with her course in life.

Coming Out To Her Family For The First Time

When Alana initially came out to her family at the age of twelve, it did not go over well. Her family did not support her, and they fought like cats and dogs for a long time. It took them over ten years from their first conversation to come around and accept her. Her parents and grandparents put her in conversion therapy, hoping it would fix her. And they clearly wasted their money.

Dealing With Racism And Discrimination

Alana has many experiences with prejudice and discrimination. For starters, early in her transition, she was scrutinized for being noticeably trans. And she didn't use the restroom on her college campus for the first year and a half because she had a counselor that told her the community wasn't ready for a trans person. She said, "where are you going to go to the bathroom? You go to the boy's room; they're going to beat you up. You go to the girl's room, and they're going to run out screaming." That terrified her, so she wouldn't use the restrooms on campus because she feared how others would react.

Additionally, she was denied a job at McDonald's because she didn't legally change her gender marker on her identification (her license and student identification had a boy's picture). Back then, she lived with her grandparents, and she did not have her own car, so she had to rely on her grandparents to take her to the DMV. Her grandparents initially didn't support or accept her, so she could not go to the DMV dressed as a woman for a new picture.

Today, Alana can navigate cisgender spaces as a presumed cis woman/people cannot tell she is trans. Thereby, the prejudice that she came across is now based on her skin color and features. Some people believe they have a right to police her, her body, and expression as a Black woman, a Brown woman, and a Caribbean person.

Undergoing Gender Confirming Surgeries And Advice

Alana has undergone gender-confirming surgeries, and her advice to others is to thoroughly do your research, find and build a community of support. Figure out who in your life can support you. It can be a blood relation, chosen family (which is often the case with the trans community), and friends. The world-wide web and social media are excellent for locating the community.

How Alana Identifies Today

Alana identifies as Caribbean or mixed. But if she had to choose one, she would say Black. She feels that she is Black passing or usually "read as Black" at first glance. Also, her experiences navigating the world have been through the lens of a Black person, which lends to her Black identity. She loves celebrating being multiracial through food. Some of her favorite foods are doubles, tamarind balls, daal, and chapati. She also enjoys various types of music and dance (dance hall, soca, bhangra, and Garba), fashion, media, and attending carnival.

Alana's Advice For Others

- Find faces like yours (e.g., Masaba Gupta, Liza Koshy, Kamala Harris, Toni Ann Singh) because this will help you see yourself personified through successful Blindian (aka Black and Indian) folks.

- Realize the beauty you possess, whether it is your skin, eyes, hair, and embrace it.

- Love your uniqueness, and do not let anyone make you feel less than proud of being who you are.

- The journey to self-love may not always be comfortable, but it is always worth it.

Alana's Advice For Parents Raising Multiracial And Transgender Children

- Teach them to love themselves.

- Show them both sides of their cultures/ethnicities so they can see the beauty and richness of both.

- Expose them to successful, influential leaders from both sides of their heritage so they know anything is possible.

- Educate them on their history because that knowledge is power.

What Alana Wishes Others Knew

Alana wish others understood the resilience of folks who live outside the margin. It is so easy to go with cultural norms and be homogenous or cisgender. But to love freely beyond culture or love yourself enough to journey outside of a cisgender identity is such a decisive move. Nevertheless, it can also be very lonely, scary, and challenging. Many multiracial people are forced to check a box and live within a label often placed on them by society. When instead, they should determine how they should identify.

Frankly put, most people do not understand the transgender community's statistics and the nearly 41% suicide rate. Being a trans woman of color represents the highest murder rate for any group in America. She cannot say enough about the importance of supporting and protecting these communities.

No, She Is Not Adopted

"She looks just like her dad."

~Bella & Kenji

Bella is Caucasian American, and her husband, Kenji, is Japanese and Filipino. They met on a free dating website. Kenji's pictures on the site were decent. Bella remembers when she met him for the first time in person thinking, "He's better looking than in the pictures." A pleasant surprise after meeting many guys on the site who were a disappointing version of their photo. While Bella knew Kenji was Asian from the first virtual contact, she did not think too much about it. Kenji shared that his ethnicity is half Japanese and half Filipino. Because he was raised in a predominately upper-class, Caucasian community, they didn't have many noticeable cultural differences.

Fast forward, to 5 years later and the birth of their beautiful half Asian and half Caucasian daughter. Her first doctor's appointment, a few days, after birth included a plethora of paperwork and the first time Bella had to mark her race. She thinks it was then that it really struck her. She started to think of the rest of her life and the multitude of events that would require one to mark a race. She does not think twice about marking white or Caucasian. Bella wondered what that would be like for her. What if she could only select one? Which would she choose? How might she be categorized or stereotyped because of her choice?

Just like many girls, Bella grew up playing house and school. She knew she wanted to grow up and get married and have kids; 3 kids in total, a girl first, and one boy. In her master plan, marriage would happen around age 22 with kids shortly after. In reality, things happened a bit more slowly, but she did have a girl first. When Oliva was born, she definitely had prominent Asian features: dark almond eyes, dark hair, and chubby cheeks. Bella spent a lot of time looking for a recognizable feature of hers. And then the comments began." She looks just like her dad!" "She has her dad's eyes!" "She has a Filipino nose; where am I thought, Bella?" She spent all this time carrying her and caring for her; which of her features did she have? Bella found baby photographs of herself and compared them. She convinced herself that they shared some qualities; that her biggest fear wouldn't come true, that people wouldn't think she was adopted when just she and Oliva were out together. Bella grew up constantly hearing that she looked just like her mom. She thinks this is why she expected she would have a daughter who would look like her. In fact, she was looking forward to it.

Is She Adopted

It took a little while, but one lovely Sunday morning at church, Bella was approached by a girl who helped with the children's ministry. She always loved seeing Oliva and helping with her. She talked about how cute she is and wanted to hold her. Then she asked the dreaded words, "Is she adopted?" As Bella told her no, that she had definitely carried her to term and birthed her, she exclaimed she only asked because she does not look like her at all. Of course, this girl has met her dad, who Oliva clearly does look like, but was not around while she was pregnant.

Another time Bella recalls being at the grocery store checkout lane with Oliva and without Kenji. The cashier noticed Oliva and asked if she was part Asian. Bella was pretty surprised. She really just sees her daughter as her unique self and thinks little about her biracial looks. As a Caucasian female, no one has ever asked her if she is white. No one asks what European countries make up her white ancestry. She wonders how Oliva's experience will be different. What obstacles might she face that she will not be able to understand, due to her being biracial?

While Bella wants her daughter to face challenges and learn resilience and problem-solving skills, racism, intolerance, and hatred are not obstacles, she wants her to face. She hopes she sees other girls at school, in the community, and in the media who look like her. She hopes she finds an American girl doll that looks like her and a baby with almond eyes and brown hair. She hopes society can continue to evolve. A friend of her once told her that she hoped she and all her siblings married and reproduced with someone of another race. She thought that would make the world more beautiful. Bella definitely agrees. She hopes Oliva has friends of many races and that she looks around and sees kids who look like her and vary greatly. Although she may not look like Bella on the outside, she plans to instill her best qualities and values in her. And she's told she already has her strong-willed, sassy attitude.

The Reality Of Being Biracial

"One's eyes serve as the windows to the world and one's mind serves as the curtains to the windows. To be able to abdicate one's biases and prejudices, emerging and embracing the beauty of what may not be akin, is to be open-minded."

~Selina

Selina comes from a diverse background; her mother is a descendent of the Black-Hawk Native Americans, who are recognized for their notorious methods of survival, courageous acts of defense, and their richness in the preservation of culture. Tracing back into her history are also Black Americans, who were initially labeled as slaves, but worked hard, struggling hand in hand, towards achieving civil rights.

Selina's father immigrated from a small third-world country in southeast Asia known as Bangladesh, where he witnessed firsthand, the traumatic events of the Indo-Pakistani War of 1971. His ancestors, known as the Nawabs, were prosperous leaders of the Persian Mughal Empire of South Asia. Most individuals may think that is intriguing. Sure, to be a part of such beautifully unique ethnic cultures is a blessing. However, such diversity facilitates alienation and micro-aggression: the unintended and indirect facilitation of racism. It creates a buffer between one's self-identity and what one is identified as.

Discovering She Is Neither All Black Nor All Indian

Imagine an innocent child; she is approximately three feet in height; she has big curly ringlets forming a mane upon her head; she is dressed in traditional Pakistani ethnic clothing, and she has henna on her hands. She is dressed up for Eid, a sacred Islamic holiday held in honor of the conclusion of Ramadan, a month of forgiveness, worship, and sacrifice. She walks into her first-grade class, where forty eyes are glued to her perceived eccentricity. Her classmates inquire is what "the red stuff" on her hands, why she is wearing 'Indian clothing', and wonder if she is even Indian.

At such a young age, Selina does not quite comprehend the inquisitiveness of her peers. However, everyone's desire to know her background triggers her thirst for knowledge about her perceived uniqueness; it is a thirst waiting to be quenched. The overwhelming inquiries and subliminal micro-aggressions stimulate a vulnerability to isolation. From this moment forward, Selina realized that she was innately, irreconcilably, different.

Too Black To Be Bangladeshi Too Bangladeshi To Be

Envision a developing adolescent, not only embarrassed by her inevitable singularity, but also propelled by the pressures of self-identification and public acceptance. Disapproving South Asians of Selina's community neglect her biracial status and display a strong racial preference, resulting in the instantaneous abandonment of her African American culture. It is exhausting having to explain why, and how she is made-up of so many diverse cultures. Being 'too Black' to be Bangladeshi and being 'too Bangladeshi' to be Black catalyzes the desertion of her cultures and the negligence towards her traditions. Selina yearns to understand herself, understand her culture, and understand how to appreciate it. To be a part of two races that are too often degraded places her at the bottom of what she perceives as the modern social caste system. She remains on her quest, in pursuits of finding a place where she 'belongs', wishing that the world could be blinded to prejudices and enlightened with embracement.

The Disappearance Of Judgement

Picture a maturing, young-adult stepping onto the foreign grounds of Bangladesh for the very first time. Hundreds of eyes gazing at her blended features cause her adrenaline to increase, and nerves to eat her alive. She climbs down from her rickshaw and walks up the endless stairs into her family's home located in Old Dhaka, also formerly known as East Pakistan. Caught by surprise, she finds fifty smiling faces, one-hundred adoring eyes, and not a slight bit of judgment. She gives all her family, whom she is meeting for the first time, her greetings. She acknowledges that unlike ever before in her lifetime, she is not being seen as, "The dark-skinned, half-Black, half-Bangladeshi girl who speaks the language of Pakistan", but as a beautiful human that is a part of a welcoming family. She comfortably speaks in her family's native language: Urdu, exchanges laughter, smiles, hugs, and for the first time, feels like she belongs. In this very moment, she realizes the beauty of her dissimilarity and the value of open-mindedness.

Society's Perception And How Selina Celebrates Being Biracial

Until this day, Selina knows that she is innately different, but she has learned that being different is not irreconcilable. Although still young, the battle she has fought with herself for over a decade in order to determine her own identity has built collective wisdom. It can be proven true that the power of diversity has the potential to build better societies. It is only those who open their minds and hearts to the artistry conveyed through diversity, that are privileged with the ability to see the world through many eyes. Conforming to society's perception of beauty is merely an exercise in palatability. Therefore, appreciating her background, culture, and divergence from the socially accepted, she will continue to advocate for those who feel as though they do not belong. Why? Because "owning one's story and loving oneself through that process is the bravest thing that one will ever do."

Selina's Advice For Parents

Expose your children to all sides of their multicultural identity. Selina's mother was raised in a Baptist Christian household, and her father was raised as a devoted Muslim. She has been exposed to both religions growing up, enjoying the festivities belonging to both sides. Her parents raised them to understand that they are indifferent to their cousins, who are either fully Black or fully Bangladeshi/Pakistani. The key to growing up mixed for her has been to understand her differences and to embrace them. Selina believes it is most important that parents expose their children to all aspects of their cultures and try to maintain as much of their unique ethnic backgrounds. Close-minded community members fear the "loss of culture," but one thing she is sure of is that she has never lost hers.s